PLUNDER
AND
BLUNDER

PLUNDER
AND
BLUNDER

THE RISE AND FALL OF
THE BUBBLE ECONOMY

DEAN BAKER

FOREWORD BY THOMAS FRANK

PoliPointPress

Production management: BookMatters
Book design: BookMatters
Cover design: Charles Kreloff

Library of Congress Cataloging-in-Publication Data
has been applied for

Published by:
PoliPointPress, LLC
P.O. Box 3008
Sausalito, CA 94966-3008
(415) 339-4100
www.p3books.com

Distributed by Ingram Publisher Services
Printed in the USA

Contents

Foreword

The economic history of the last decade is the history of asset bubbles. The pattern repeats itself again and again: the same industries, the same millennial rhetoric, the same crooked insider behavior, sometimes even the same individual players. Each time we convince ourselves that this is it, that tech stocks are going to make us all millionaires, that real estate never goes down but only goes up, and up, and up.

So the bubbles expand and burst, leaving trillions of dollars of destruction in their wake, and yet we refuse to recognize the essential similarity between the first one and the second one and, surely, the third one, which will no doubt take us all in a few years down the road.

Dean Baker's contribution is to point out not only the essential similarity between the dot-com bubble and the real-estate bubble, but also to historicize the phenomenon. For forty years after the end of World War II, asset bubbles were insignificant, while blue-collar workers participated in the country's prosperity alongside shareholders. Boom and bust were leveled out by a variety of regulatory devices.

With the atavistic economic policies of the Reagan, Clinton, and Bush years, however, the old ways have returned. Money flows irresistibly to the top, and along the way oversight is muted or compromised in some manner, professional ethics cease to restrain, conflicts of interest run rampant, and government becomes the property of those who can afford it. The accountants don't detect Enron's massive debts, and the bond ratings agencies miss the dangers of subprime mortgages. Firms backing the dot-coms press dot-com stock on their clients, even as the home appraisers work in confederation with the real-estate industry. The SEC simply misses the whole thing, while the chieftains of the Federal Reserve pooh-pooh the idea of an overheated real-estate market.

Accountability is as passé as independent-minded corporate boards. And not just in matters of executive compensation. Idiocy prevails from top to bottom. Managers book bogus profits to pad their own paychecks and eventually drive their companies into bankruptcy. Workers are laid off by the thousands; the managers who never saw disaster coming retreat to their castles with $100 million packages. Meanwhile, in the larger culture, we take stock-picking (and political) advice from the authors of *Dow 36,000*; we take real-estate advice from the author of a book called *Why the Real Estate Boom Will Not Bust*. Our most esteemed professional economists get it wrong again and again, and yet their day of reckoning never seems to come. The culture has been gamed as thoroughly as the financial system.

Dean Baker is one of those who got it right, and in this book he tells us exactly what we must do to stop the cycle from repeating itself yet again. Deflating bubbles must become one of the chief economic priorities of our regulatory system, and that system itself must be rebuilt, essentially, from the bottom up.

This time, let's listen to the man.

Thomas Frank

Introduction

For the second time this decade, the economy is sinking into a recession due to the collapse of a financial bubble. The housing collapse is likely to produce a recession that's far deeper and longer than the 2001 downturn caused by the stock-market crash. Because many more families own homes than have large stock portfolios, the collapse of the housing bubble is likely to affect the economic security of many more Americans. In short, this is a huge deal.

Good policy can ease the economic pain of the crash, but the tragic part of this story is how preventable it was. As was the case with the stock bubble, any competent expert should have recognized—and warned against—the housing bubble.

This is especially true for experts in policy positions, such as Federal Reserve Board Chairman Alan Greenspan and top officials in the Bush administration. Nothing they were doing between 2002 and 2006 was more important than reining in the housing bubble. Instead, they cheered it on, celebrating the growth in housing wealth and homeownership.

The failure was not just in government. Top executives in the **financial sector*** fueled the housing bubble in ways that probably would have landed less prominent citizens in jail. These executives pocketed vast sums of money while pushing their companies toward or into bankruptcy. While millions of families face the loss of their homes, and tens of millions have seen their life's savings evaporate with the plunge in home prices, most of the financiers responsible for this disaster remain fabulously rich.

The failure was also in the economics profession. With extremely few exceptions, economists ignored the growth of an $8 trillion housing bubble—an average of $110,000 for every homeowner in the country. For the most part, economists who focused on the housing market denied that any bubble existed. Their colleagues were more concerned with other problems: for example, the possibility that we might have to raise Social Security taxes in 40 years. (Never mind the fact that we did so in every decade between the 1950s and the 1990s.)

---

*The first instance of economic terms whose definitions can be found in the glossary are shown in a **bold typeface**.

A lack of attention to the housing bubble didn't stop top economists from praising the leading policymakers. In 2005, when the housing bubble was inflating rapidly, central bankers paid tribute to Alan Greenspan at their annual meeting in Jackson Hole, Wyoming. One paper discussed the proposition that Greenspan was the greatest central banker of all time.

One other group—the media—figures prominently in this story. Key news outlets presented the bubble promoters as experts on the economy. Even the most extreme bubble celebrants could count on a respectful hearing in these circles. James Glassman, coauthor of *Dow 36,000: The New Strategy for Profiting from the Coming Rise in the Stock Market*, was a regular columnist for the *Washington Post,* as well as a guest on the *NewsHour with Jim Lehrer,* in the months just before the stock market's 2000 crash. David Lereah, chief economist of the National Association of Realtors and the author of *Why the Real Estate Boom Will Not Bust and How You Can Profit from It*, was the most widely cited housing expert in major media outlets during the peak years of the housing bubble. Careful readers of the most respected newspapers and viewers of the top-rated news shows saw little information suggesting that stock prices in the late 1990s were seriously overvalued, or that real estate prices in this decade could fall sharply.

In short, the story of these financial bubbles is a tale of major institutional failures. The top corporate actors enriched themselves even as they drove their companies toward bankruptcy. The Federal Reserve Board and other regulatory institutions largely sat on the sidelines. Economists and the media promoted these bubbles, or at least ignored the danger of them popping.

This book is an effort to understand how these bubbles developed and how future financial disasters can be prevented. It is not an exercise in 20/20 hindsight. As I will show, it was possible to recognize these bubbles in time to avert them. A few of us did warn Americans about the likelihood of the problems we're facing now. We didn't have the same megaphone as a Federal Reserve Board chairman, a Treasury secretary, or even a *Washington Post* columnist, so these warnings had relatively little impact. But it would be wrong to conclude, as many would have us believe now, that it was beyond our ability to predict or avert these market meltdowns.

Beneath all the surface complexity of our current mess lies a basic story—not only of institutional failure, but also of energetic self-deception. Grasping that story is the first step toward preventing the next economic calamity.

CHAPTER 1

How We Got Here

There's nothing natural or inevitable about financial bubbles. They aren't like hurricanes or earthquakes. In fact, the stock- and housing-market bubbles of the last decade are largely the culmination of very human policy choices that began in the early 1980s.

For most of the three decades before that, the U.S. economy was strong and on solid ground. Between 1947 and 1973, the economy grew steadily, productivity increased rapidly, and the unemployment rate was low. Moreover, the benefits of that economic growth were shared widely. The real income of the typical family, for example, rose at a 2.8 percent annual rate during this time.[1] Given this record, most Americans believed that their children would have better opportunities than they did.

There were other signs of growing affluence. The share of families that owned homes rose from 55 percent in 1950 to over 64 percent in 1973. (Since then, the homeownership rate has only inched up modestly.) Cars became standard household items even for people with relatively modest incomes. At the beginning of the period, just over half of all families owned a car. By 1973, more than 83 percent of families did.[2]

Rapid **productivity growth** was the key to this broad prosperity. To appreciate the magnitude of this growth, consider the following: if we maintained the same rate of productivity growth the United States experienced in the early postwar era, we would be able to take an additional 24 weeks of vacation each year, or reduce our average workweek to 21 hours, and still have the same income in 2030 as we do today.

The postwar period had its social problems, so we shouldn't idealize it. In much of the country, racial segregation was entrenched in law until the mid-1960s and in social reality long after that. African Americans, Latinos, and other minority groups faced overt discrimination in employment, education, and housing. Discrimination based on gender and sexual orientation was standard practice, though the movements challenging such discrimination gained enormous strength through the 1960s and 1970s.

Despite these social problems, it was possible to say that things were getting better, at least economically. Broad prosperity worked for America. In addition to helping more families, it produced a kind of virtuous circle. Productivity gains were passed on to workers in the form of wage growth. Higher wages led to more consumption, which encouraged companies to invest in new plants and equipment. That investment increased productivity, which provided the basis for further wage growth. In this way, growth fed upon itself.

The stock market rose during this postwar period, but it never drove the economy. In the aftermath of the Great Depression, when Americans were more ambivalent about stock ownership, the percentage of Americans with stock portfolios grew gradually, as did public and private sector pension funds. By the end of the 1970s, these funds owned 18.5 percent of the stock market.[3] But the vast majority of Americans still had no other direct stake in the stock market. Their savings were mostly held in traditional pension plans or in old-fashioned savings accounts.

This was also a period of expanding home construction. An average of 1.56 million units were added to the housing stock each year between 1959 and 1973. Increases in home values in many parts of the country exceeded the overall rate of inflation, but many cities (including Detroit, Cleveland, and St. Louis) lost jobs and population, and house prices decreased there. On balance, inflation-adjusted house prices for the country as a whole actually fell by 12 percent between 1953 and 1973.[4] The country had solid growth and prosperity by any measure, but that growth wasn't driven by runaway real estate values.

The economy in those decades differed from the economy today in other important ways. At that time, the U.S. economy was far more insulated from international competition. Imports on average ranged from 4.2 percent of **gross domestic product (GDP)** in the 1950s to 7.6 percent in 1970. Much of that increase was due to the rise in oil prices. By 2007, the import share of GDP exceeded 17 percent.

In the early post–World War II period, the U.S. financial sector played a comparatively small role in the economy. This sector accounted for less than 6 percent of corporate profits in the late 1940s and averaged less than 10 percent in the 1960s. In its peak year in 2004, however, the financial sector accounted for more than 30 percent of corporate profits (see figure 1.1).

Part of the extraordinary growth in the financial sector was due to a simple rearrangement of tasks. Financial activities formerly carried out by the nonfinancial sector were contracted out to separate firms in the financial sector. For example, many small stores used to extend credit to their customers and send them monthly bills. Credit cards like MasterCard and Visa largely displaced this sort of store-based credit in the 1970s and 1980s, shifting profits from retail stores to companies in the

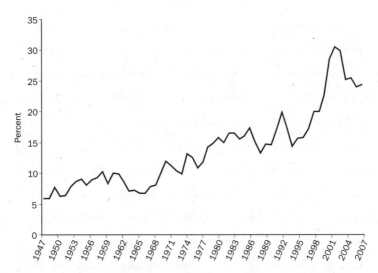

FIGURE 1.1 Financial Sector Share of Domestic Corporate Profits

Source: Bureau of Economic Analysis, National Income and Product Accounts.

financial sector. Similarly, it became more common for non-financial businesses to outsource accounting and various types of money management activities. This trend increased the size of the financial sector relative to the nonfinancial sector.

But the financial sector didn't grow only for these reasons. With the increase of computer power, the expansion of deregulation, and the internationalization of financial markets, the financial sector developed a qualitatively different character and became a major economic force in its own right.

Cheap computing power allowed for the proliferation of complex financial instruments that were previously impractical. For example, new forms of information technology made it easier to create **options** on a wide range of **commodities** and financial products, including stocks, treasury bonds, and currencies. These options, in turn, could provide a relatively low-cost form of insurance to companies and investors. For example, an investor who wanted to protect herself from the possibility that her shares of General Electric stock would fall in price could buy an option that gave her the right to sell her stock at a specific price. If the price of General Electric stock plummeted, the investor could take advantage of the option and protect herself against most of the loss. Of course, she would lose the cost of the option if the share price didn't fall, but insurance isn't free.

Such options provided a mechanism for placing highly **leveraged** bets, in which even small investors could rack up large gains or losses. As **derivative markets** expanded in the 1980s and 1990s, it became standard practice for companies to use these instruments to insure themselves against a wide range of possible risks, such as rises in commodity prices, fluctuations in currency values or interest rates, and defaults by borrowers. Speculators also used these instruments to make bets with large potential payoffs and risks. The most successful of these speculators accumulated vast fortunes on these highly leveraged bets.

Especially after the election of Ronald Reagan in 1980, many business interests and policymakers pushed successfully for the deregulation of financial and other markets. Many of the rules governing financial markets had been put in place after the financial abuses of the 1920s, which led up to the Great Depression. Deregulation or weakened enforcement meant that the old lines between commercial banks, investment banks, and insurance companies were blurred or disappeared altogether. Deregulation proponents argued that outmoded regulations put an unnecessary drag on financial markets, but in some cases, the deregulation efforts were even more costly. The deregulation of savings and loan institutions in the 1980s led to the failure of over 2,400 U.S. thrift institutions and cost about $560 billion, most of which was ultimately paid for by U.S. taxpayers. The bailout also contributed to the large federal budget deficits of the early 1990s.

Despite these high-profile debacles, the deregulatory zeal remained undiminished. The enforcement of clear boundaries between financial sectors weakened during this time, and the Glass-Steagall Act, which mandated separation between investment banks and commercial banks, was finally repealed in 1999. This allowed financial giants to operate in new markets and grow even larger.

The internationalization of financial markets also meant that vast pools of investment capital were made available to a new kind of financial operator. Previously, small and midsize firms might be taken over by outside investors, but these new sources of capital made it possible for relatively small groups of investors to take over even the largest firms. Takeover artists like Carl Icahn and T. Boone Pickens managed to buy up companies almost entirely with borrowed money. In these **leveraged buyouts (LBOs)**, the new management tried to cuts costs or sell off assets quickly to reduce its debt. Often the cost-cutting involved big layoffs, substantial pay cuts for remaining workers, and confrontations with labor unions. Frank Lorenzo, who specialized in airline takeovers, frequently sought such confrontations and replaced striking union workers with nonunion employees.

Several of the largest U.S. corporations were taken over through LBOs in the 1980s. If an LBO worked, the takeover artist took the company public again and sold shares for a large gain. If it didn't work, the company often went bankrupt, as was the case with several airlines taken over by Lorenzo.

With the advent of such takeovers, corporations changed the way they did business. Because they were vulnerable to takeovers any time their stock price dipped, corporate managers became far more concerned about daily share prices. Also, companies had to emulate the practices of the LBOs. A company that showed low profitability might trim its workforce for fear that it would be bought up by outside investors, who would then take this step themselves.

TRICKLE-UP ECONOMICS

After 1973, the U.S. economy began to change in other important ways. First, the extraordinary productivity growth of the postwar era came to an end. Economists are still debating the reasons for this productivity slowdown that began in 1973 and continued into the 1980s. One important factor was a huge increase in oil prices. Another likely factor was increased competition from Europe and Japan, whose economies had by then fully recovered from the destruction of World War II.

Whatever the causes, the slowdown in productivity growth meant that wage growth also stagnated. The typical family still saw rising income during this period, but much of that increase was the result of women entering the labor force in large numbers. The proliferation of two-paycheck families both masked and responded to that period's sluggish productivity and wage growth.

Something else changed in the U.S. economy after 1980. In the 1970s, the benefits of productivity growth, though small, were still shared more or less evenly. In the 1980s, productivity growth remained weak, but the benefits of that growth began to go almost exclusively to those at the top of the income ladder.

This upward redistribution of income was largely the result of conscious policy changes. One such change was the Reagan administration's campaign to weaken unions. That campaign had several different facets. First, the administration appointed people to the National Labor Relations Board (NLRB) who were markedly more pro-management than appointees of previous presidents of either party.[5] The Reagan administration also reduced funding to the NLRB, so that it developed a large backlog of cases. This meant that workers who filed complaints might wait years for their cases to be heard.

In 1981, Reagan also took the extraordinary step of firing striking air traffic controllers and replacing them with their military counterparts. He had the legal authority to take this action, because strikes by federal workers are illegal. But previous strikes by public sector employees hadn't led to mass firings. Soon, other major employers took the step of firing striking workers, and many other employers used this threat to end or head off strikes. As a result, unions lost much of their bargaining power.

Reagan also blocked increases in the minimum wage during his presidency. As a result, the real value of the minimum wage was eroded each year by inflation. In real terms, the minimum wage was 26 percent lower when Reagan left office in 1989 than when he took office in 1981.

Another Reagan policy indirectly undermined the living standards of middle-class workers. The large federal budget deficits of the Reagan years, coupled with the high interest rate policy pursued by the Federal Reserve Board, caused the dollar to rise in value against the currencies of our major trading partners. The higher dollar made imports from these countries relatively cheap for American consumers, but it also made it harder for American firms to sell their products abroad. This in turn led to the loss of many high-wage jobs in manufacturing, especially in the automobile and steel sectors.

Trade agreements signed in the 1990s also contributed to the upward redistribution of income. NAFTA (North American Free Trade Agreement) and other pacts were explicitly designed to put U.S. manufacturing workers in direct competition with low-paid workers in the developing world. In effect, NAFTA helped transfer U.S. manufacturing capacity to Mexico. Again, this was a conscious policy decision. Imagine what would have happened if, in the name of free trade, a deal was struck to put our most highly educated professionals—doctors, lawyers, and dentists, for example—in direct competition with their much lower-paid counterparts in the developing world. That would put downward pressure on their earnings, just as current trade deals put downward pressure on the earnings of blue-collar American workers.

Immigration policy has also been structured and enforced in a way that widens income gaps. Specifically, the lax enforcement of immigration laws amounts to an implicit policy of allowing undocumented immigrants to work in low-paying jobs. By increasing the supply of low-wage labor, this policy drives down wages for native-born workers who might otherwise hold these jobs. Again, less-educated American workers have faced competition in the labor market, even though the most highly educated workers have been largely protected.

Taken together, these policy changes hurt average American workers. Between 1980 and 1995, their real wages declined 0.9 percent. For workers lower down the income ladder, the situation was even worse. Workers at the 30th percentile of the wage distribution saw their wages decline by 2.7 percent after adjusting for inflation. Workers at the 10th percentile had a 7.5 percent decline in real wages over this period.

Other Americans profited handsomely during this time. Some of the big winners were professionals, CEOs, and Wall Street fund managers. The pay of CEOs went from 24 times the pay of a typical worker in 1965 to 300 times the pay of a typical worker in 2000.[6] This change was due to the breakdown in the **corporate governance structures** that had previously kept CEO pay in check. The top executives of major corporations were answerable to boards of directors, whom they often appointed. Corporate boards and compensation committees dished out sweetheart contracts to their allies, even when the performance of many of these executives should have earned them a pink slip. Wall Street fund managers did even better than CEOs, with the most highly paid among them earning hundreds of millions of dollar in good years. But even in the bad years, many fund managers made out fine.

The upward redistribution of income after 1980 meant that the economy couldn't sustain the same virtuous circle that characterized the postwar period. Wages weren't rising consistently, so workers couldn't buy more with their income. Even with more two-paycheck households, many families saved less and borrowed more to support their standard of living. The increased globalization of the economy, especially in the manufacturing sector, meant a weaker connection between increases in domestic demand and increases in investment in new U.S. plants and equipment. American firms could meet increases in demand with production from abroad, and many did. In short, policy changes during this period helped break the virtuous circle of rising productivity, wages, consumption, and investment.

More and more, the U.S. economy depended on something

far less virtuous than productivity gains and broad prosperity. In pursuit of short-term growth, key institutions relied on risky bets and unsustainable policies. In short, we got hooked on bubbles.

CHAPTER 2

The Clinton Era and the Origins of the Stock Bubble

The bubble economy began to take shape in the mid-1990s, when America saw the first years of sustained prosperity in two decades. Most of the economic signs were pointing in the right direction. In 1997, the unemployment rate fell below 5 percent for the first time in more than two decades, and the economy added an average of 3 million jobs every year from 1996 until 2001. Better yet, wages were rising at all levels of the income ladder. In spite of this strong wage growth, inflation was well contained until energy prices began to rise in 2000.

This prosperity was made possible in part by a strong uptick in productivity growth. Between 1973 and 1995, the annual rate of such growth averaged just 1.5 percent, a little more than half the rate of the postwar period. But in late 1995, the rate of productivity growth increased. From that point to the onset of recession in 2001, the annual rate of productivity growth averaged 2.4 percent. For much of the country, the economy of the late 1990s looked like its 1947–1973 counterpart.

It's widely believed that this prosperity was a direct outgrowth of the Clinton administration's policies, especially its efforts to reduce the federal budget deficit. According to this account, deficit reduction drove down interest rates, which in turn sparked investment. Increased investment led to a boom in productivity, which allowed the country to enjoy the first period of sustained low unemployment and broad-based wage growth since the early 1970s. But everything turned sour, the story goes, when President Bush took office, cut taxes, and began running deficits. Those deficits ended the productivity boom and eventually started undermining confidence in the dollar. The end result was recession and higher inflation due to oil price hikes and the falling dollar.

This account, though widely credited, is almost completely at odds with reality. The growth burst of the late 1990s had little to do with deficit reduction (at least directly) and had everything to do with two unsustainable bubbles—the stock-market and an overvalued dollar. To understand those bubbles, we have to take a critical look at the conventional wisdom and understand what was actually happening in the economy during the 1990s.

THE CLINTON GAME PLAN

When President Clinton came into office in 1993, he promised to pursue two conflicting agendas. The first was his "public investment" agenda, centered on promoting investment in infrastructure, research and development, and education and training. This position was most strongly identified with Labor Secretary Robert Reich. The second agenda was to reduce the federal budget deficit. This position was most strongly associated with then Treasury Secretary Lloyd Bentsen and Robert Rubin, the head of Clinton's newly created National Economic Council.

The public investment agenda had proven very popular during the presidential campaign. Clinton's economic manifesto was titled "Putting People First," and it highlighted his plans to invest in the country and its people. Clinton drew an explicit contrast in this respect with independent candidate Ross Perot, who made deficit reduction the centerpiece of his campaign and eventually received almost 19 percent of the vote. Once the election was over, however, the Bentsen and Rubin initiative quickly took precedence over the public investment campaign, and the Clinton administration gave priority to the deficit reduction agenda. Reich sought to press his case for public investment, but he was outnumbered and outmaneuvered. For his part, President Clinton declined to take up the cause. As Reich commented on his efforts, "I am addressing a sleeping President."[1]

There has been extensive research on the economic impacts of reducing the federal budget deficit. The overall conclusion of that research is that deficit reduction provides only a modest boost to economic growth. Moreover, that modest boost will be visible only over the long term. The Clinton team was aware of this. In the 1994 *Economic Report of the President*, it used a standard model to project gains from the sort of deficit reduction envisioned in the president's initial budget. After ten years, real wages would be approximately 2 percent higher than in the baseline case. This is a difference of approximately 0.2 percentage points annually in the projected growth path. Even the cumulative effects after a decade would barely be visible to anyone who didn't track the economy for a living. Furthermore, because deficit reduction would require higher taxes, the model didn't project consumption to rise even to its **baseline path** until the fifth year.[2]

Another predicted outcome of lower budget deficits was a fall in the value of the dollar. In fact, the dollar continued a decline in real value against most major currencies during the early years of the Clinton administration. To economists, the drop in the dollar was perhaps the most important outcome of deficit reduction. The trade deficit had exploded to more than 3 percent of GDP in the mid-1980s as a result of a sharp run-up in the dollar. This run-up was attributed to high U.S. interest rates, which were in turn attributed to the high budget deficits of the early Reagan years.[3] When the dollar continued its downward path through the first three years of the Clinton administration, experts generally viewed that development as positive.

What, then, did the Clinton administration expect from cutting the budget deficit? The plan was that a lower deficit would lead to lower interest rates, which would lead to increases in the consumption of durable goods (for example, cars and washing machines), residential construction, and business investment. By lowering the value of the dollar, the Clinton approach would also increase net exports and cut the trade deficit. All of these projected effects of the Clinton plan were relatively short term. Nothing in the standard models used by the Clinton administration suggested that deficit reduction would lead to large increases in the rate of productivity or overall GDP growth.

THE EARLY RESULTS

The economic results in the first years of the Clinton administration were mixed. The economy grew at a respectable pace in both 1993 and 1994, but wages were barely keeping pace with inflation. Durable goods spending did rise sharply, as people purchased cars and computers at a rapid rate. Investment was increasing, but it was mostly offsetting the downturn associated with the 1990–1991 recession. Productivity growth was sluggish—an average of 0.7 percent per year for the first three years of Clinton's presidency.

Enter Alan Greenspan, the Federal Reserve chairman appointed by Ronald Reagan in 1987. Under Alan Greenspan's leadership, the Fed agreed to pursue a relatively loose monetary policy during the Clinton years in exchange for progress on deficit reduction.[4] Greenspan held the short-term **federal funds rate** at 3 percent—the lowest level since the 1960s—through 1993 and into 1994. Mortgage rate reductions boosted the economy both directly and indirectly. In particular, they made it easier to finance house purchases, which helped the housing sector and allowed millions of homeowners to get out of higher-priced mortgages through refinancing. Housing construction increased at just under a 9 percent annual rate in 1993–1994. This was a good result, but hardly earth-shattering. In the first two years after the much steeper recession of the early 1980s, housing expanded at an annual rate of more than 25 percent.

If the economy's performance in the first two years of the Clinton administration was unremarkable, things began to change in the third year. Initially, the economy began to slow. This trend was the result of a deliberate policy. Greenspan had begun raising interest rates in February 1994, and by March 1995, he had pushed the federal funds rate from 3 to 6 percent. Greenspan's rationale was that the unemployment rate was falling toward the "non-accelerating inflation rate of unemployment" (NAIRU), which at that time was thought to range between 5.6 and 6.4 percent.

Experts considered NAIRU a key benchmark. If the unemployment rate fell below it, workers might demand wage increases that outstripped productivity growth. Firms would pass on these wage increases in the form of higher prices, which in turn would cause workers to demand still larger wage increases in future bargaining. The result would be an **inflationary spiral.**

To head off this spiral, Greenspan raised interest rates. He then led the Fed in a remarkable move. He lowered the federal funds rate in the summer of 1995, arguing that the economy could grow more rapidly than most economists believed because productivity growth wasn't being measured accurately. In Greenspan's view, more rapid growth wouldn't necessarily push the unemployment rate below the NAIRU.[5]

Other Fed members objected to Greenspan's policy. Clinton's two most prominent appointees to the Federal Reserve Board, Janet Yellen and Lawrence Meyer, argued strenuously against Greenspan. They insisted on the conventional NAIRU story and argued that inflation would increase if Greenspan let the unemployment rate fall further. But Greenspan's extraordinary stature prevailed. The Fed lowered rates, and the economy began to grow more rapidly. In the year from the second quarter of 1995 through the second quarter of 1996, growth averaged almost 4 percent.

Greenspan was onto something. The rate of productivity growth over this period was 3 percent, an extraordinary pace for a period in which the economy wasn't recovering from a recession. Few economists had anticipated this upturn, and there was little agreement as to what caused it or whether it would continue. But it appeared that Greenspan had been right to let the economy grow more rapidly. The unemployment rate continued to edge lower, but no uptick in the inflation rate was evidenced, even though wages were finally beginning to outpace inflation.

Another policy change during this time concerned the value of the dollar relative to other currencies. The Clinton administration's low-dollar approach shifted when Robert Rubin became Treasury secretary in January 1995. Rubin argued that a strong dollar helped to control inflation and raise living standards. This is true, at least in the short run, but a high dollar can't be sustained over the long run. It lowers the price of imports for American consumers and makes U.S. exports more costly to foreign consumers. With more imports and fewer exports, the trade deficit rises. This large trade deficit—the inevitable outcome of Rubin's policy—eventually forces down the value of the dollar, unless foreigners can be persuaded to lend an ever-increasing amount of money to the United States. This drop in the dollar means rising import prices, higher inflation, and lower living standards. In other words, by pumping up the dollar in the short term, the Clinton administration was helping to create the bubble economy.

THE BEGINNING
OF THE BUBBLE ECONOMY

Policy changes were one part of the economic growth story of the 1990s, but other developments were even more important. One was that computers were finally having the transformative effect on society that had long been predicted. The use of personal computers was exploding, both at home and at work, and the Web was coming into widespread use. These developments led to an outpouring of enthusiasm, much of it not well-grounded, about the potential for the "new economy."

This giddiness, in turn, affected the stock market. The broadly based S&P 500 index rose 33.5 percent through 1995, and then climbed another 13.5 percent in 1996. The narrower but more widely publicized Dow Jones Industrial index also rose by 33.5 percent in 1995 and added another 26 percent to this gain in 1996. But the really big gains were on the

NASDAQ index, where the new-economy technology companies were listed. This index rose 41.7 percent in 1995 and 22.1 percent in 1996.

In December 1996, Alan Greenspan famously commented on the stock market's "irrational exuberance." He quickly qualified his remark, but the basis for his comment was real. The **price-to-earnings (PE) ratio** for the S&P 500 was almost 20 to 1, far above the historic average of 14.5 to 1. That meant that the soaring stock prices weren't tightly connected to corporate profits. In media coverage of this period, the stock price run-up was just one more piece of good news; anyone who thought it was a problem was virtually excluded from public debate.

When voters re-elected President Clinton in 1996, the economy was a major factor. The world looked much better to most workers than it had four years earlier. With the unemployment rate hovering near 5 percent, a low rate by recent standards, the stronger labor market was finally allowing for some modest wage growth. Furthermore, the decline in interest rates—a direct result of the deficit reduction package—helped millions of homeowners refinance at lower rates. Like any good politician, President Clinton took credit for the economic gains during his first term, but the economic takeoff in 1995 had more to do with the rate of productivity growth than his program of deficit reduction, which at best was expected to have a modest impact.

Shortly after Clinton's re-election, the stock market took off again. The real value of the Dow Jones Industrial Average rose by 22.6 percent in 1997 and another 16.1 percent in 1998. The S&P 500 gained 31 percent in 1997 and 26.7 percent in 1998. The NASDAQ again topped the charts, rising by 40.2 percent in 1998, after a relatively meager 21.7 percent rise in 1997. Many otherwise intelligent people became obsessed with the stock market. They followed the minute-by-minute movements of the Dow or the NASDAQ on their computers, on various portable phone devises, or on cable business channels.

While reporting on the stock market, the so-called responsible media treated many cheerleaders as if they were serious experts. Those who raised questions about the stock price bubble were virtually nonexistent in the *New York Times,* the *Washington Post,* NPR, and other major news outlets. This uncritical reporting and lack of differing perspectives contributed to the irrational exuberance Greenspan had briefly cited.

The stock market surge turned the economy upside down. New technology startups quickly had stock valuations in the billions, dwarfing those of the established giants of the old economy. Yahoo! Inc., the Internet services firm, had a **market capitalization** of $140 billion at its peak in 2000. By comparison, the market capitalization of USX, the country's largest steel company, fell to $1.5 billion the same year, and J.C. Penny's market capitalization dropped to $1.9 billion.

Much of the Internet stock wealth quickly vanished in the subsequent crash of 2000–2002, but the run-up in stock prices created significant imbalances in the economy. Households, pension fund managers, foundations, and other investors were handing over real money for stock that commanded enormous value at the time. The result for many of these investors was a huge loss of wealth—and **windfall profits** for those smart enough to benefit while the bubble lasted or lucky enough to get out before the collapse.

TWO CASES IN POINT

The experiences of two companies illustrate the nature of both this bubble and the official responses to it. In 2000, America Online (subsequently AOL), then the leading provider of dial-up Internet services, saw its stock valuation soar to $190 billion. It arranged to buy out Time-Warner in an **all-stock transaction**. At the time, the price of the media giant was put at $97 billion.

The value of AOL stock quickly plummeted in the wake of the stock market crash and the growth of high-speed Internet services that replaced dial-up. Even so, Steven Case, the founder and chairman of AOL, became incredibly wealthy. According to *Forbes* list of the 400 wealthiest Americans, Case's net worth came to more than $1.4 billion in 2001. Had he held his AOL stock through the crash, he would have ended up with a small fraction of that wealth.

The Time-Warner shareholders were considerably less lucky. They effectively handed over most of the value of Time-Warner to Steven Case and the other AOL shareholders. The other losers in that deal included many middle-class employees who held the Time-Warner stock directly or indirectly through their retirement funds. Gerald Levin, the CEO of Time-Warner, who arranged the sale, retained all of the compensation and bonuses he had amassed. Likewise, most of the fund managers who squandered the wealth of their clients suffered no serious career or financial consequences themselves.

Another company's story presaged the official response to the bubble. One of the most successful **hedge funds** of the period was the Long-Term Capital Management Fund, which was started in 1994 by John Meriwether, a former vice president and head of bond trading at Salomon Brothers. Its board included Myron Scholes and Robert Merton, both Nobel Prize winners who had done pathbreaking work in finance theory.

From its inception, the fund produced annual returns in the neighborhood of 40 percent. Its strategy was to pursue highly leveraged **arbitrage bets**, expecting that the market would eventually eliminate seemingly irrational gaps in price in different places. For example, the fund saw an arbitrage opportunity in the fact that shares of the oil company Royal Dutch Shell, which is listed on both the Netherlands stock exchange and the U.S. stock exchange, sold for more on the Netherlands exchange than on the U.S. exchange. Long-Term Capital bet that the price of shares of Shell in the Netherlands would fall. It also bought shares in the United States, thereby betting that U.S. prices would rise. If the prices of the shares in the Netherlands and U.S. stock markets converged, Long-Term Capital could win on both sides.

This approach ran into problems in the summer of 1998, when the Russian financial crisis disrupted normal trading patterns on which Long-Term Capital was counting. In many instances, Long-Term Capital had bet that prices would converge, but they continued to diverge. For example, the price of Shell stock in the Netherlands and the United States moved further apart. Instead of winning on both sides of its bet, Long-Term Capital was losing, and because its bets were highly leveraged, the company quickly found itself facing insolvency.

At this point, Alan Greenspan stepped in. Rather than allow Long-Term Capital to enter bankruptcy, Greenspan asked its major creditors to inject new capital into the firm. This would allow Long-Term Capital to maintain its investment positions and gradually sell them off. Greenspan's concern was that if Long-Term Capital was forced to sell off its holdings immediately, **panic selling** might cause a downward spiral in the price of certain assets, leading to large and potentially dan-gerous losses for major banks.

Greenspan's intervention raised two important issues. First, it showed that the Fed was concerned about low asset prices. From the standpoint of the economy as a whole, there's no more reason to be concerned about underpriced assets than about overpriced ones. Both will lead to distortions in the economy. By his actions, Greenspan indicated that he thought he knew better than the market what those asset prices should be. He also showed that he was prepared to use the Fed's power to prevent the market from pushing those prices down. That was a huge favor to the creditors of Long-Term Capital, who reaped benefits from the services of the country's central bank at no cost.

The other issue raised by the Fed's intervention is what it signaled to investors about the risks they were taking and what the consequences might be. Greenspan may have been correct in his assessment that the unraveling of Long-Term Capital would lead to panic selling. Investors presumably knew that they faced this risk. But they also learned something new: that Greenspan was willing to coordinate the activities of major banks to prevent such a run. This new knowledge reassured investors that Greenspan was watching out for them. After saving the banks who had lent money to Long-Term Capital from themselves, Greenspan neither implemented changes nor requested any from Congress to prevent another meltdown. All of this together gave investors a clear green light to take even bigger risks.

THE ECONOMY
IN THE LATE BUBBLE YEARS

As good as the economy looked when Bill Clinton ran for re-election in 1996, it was looking even better by 2000. For the first time since the late 1960s, the unemployment rate had fallen below 5 percent for a sustained period, creating the basis for real wage gains among income groups at all wage levels.

Low unemployment rates are especially beneficial for the most disadvantaged segments of society. As a rule of thumb, the unemployment rate for African Americans is twice the overall unemployment rate; for African American teens, it's six times the overall rate. The unemployment rate for Latinos tends to be approximately 1.5 times the overall level.

The low unemployment rate of the late 1990s gave these groups an extraordinary opportunity to experience real economic gains—an opportunity they had not seen in more than a quarter century (see figure 2.1). An unemployment rate of 24 percent for black teens may sound bleak, but it hovered near 40 percent earlier in the 1990s and was greater than 50 percent in the 1980s.

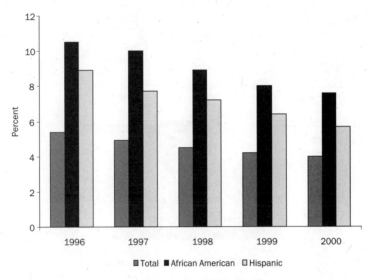

FIGURE 2.1 Unemployment Rates, 1996–2000

Source: Bureau of Labor Statistics.

Other indicators were going in the right direction, too. There were gains in real family income for African Americans and Latinos (see figure 2.2), and the homeownership rate for African Americans rose from 42.3 percent in 1994 to 47.2 percent in 2000.

Although the unemployment rate fell to levels that most economists believed would trigger inflation, no such inflation materialized. The core inflation rate for 2000 was just 2.6 percent, the same rate as in 1994, the year when the unemployment rate first fell under the conventional estimates of the NAIRU.

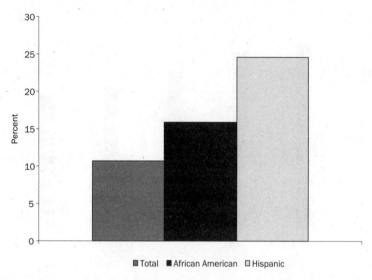

FIGURE 2.2 Gains in Real Median Family Income, 1995–2000
Source: Bureau of Labor Statistics.

The overall inflation rate rose from 2.7 percent in 1999 to 3.4 percent in 2000, but the main cause was higher worldwide energy prices, not low unemployment in the United States, and even this higher inflation rate was virtually identical to the 3.3 percent rate in 1996. Whether the conventional view of the NAIRU was simply wrong or some structural change had occurred in the 1990s, that view couldn't explain the relationship between inflation and unemployment during this period.

What did explain the economic good news during this period? The key factor was the uptick in productivity growth, which continued until the middle of 2004. Why this speed-up began in the mid-1990s is unclear, but it certainly isn't attributable to deficit reduction or other Clinton policies. As mentioned earlier, the conventional story of the Clinton years is belied by a host of economic facts. There's little evidence to support the view that deficit reduction led to lower interest rates, increased investment, productivity growth, and wage gains. In fact, a great deal of the deficit reduction was attributable to an unexpected surge in tax revenue, which was largely due to capital gains from the stock bubble that was forming during this time. Without that stock bubble, it's unlikely that Clinton would have balanced the budget, much less run large surpluses.

Another problem with the conventional story of the Clinton years is that real interest rates remained at historically high levels (see figure 2.3). The declines in the real mortgage rate and the real corporate bond rate were just 0.6 and 0.7 percentage points, respectively, and these rates remained several percentage points higher than their levels in the 1960s and 1970s. With real interest rates changing little, the rise in investment was limited.

What did increase markedly, especially when compared to earlier booms, was consumption. That trend was supported by the Clinton administration's high-dollar policy, which made foreign goods cheaper for American consumers. The problem

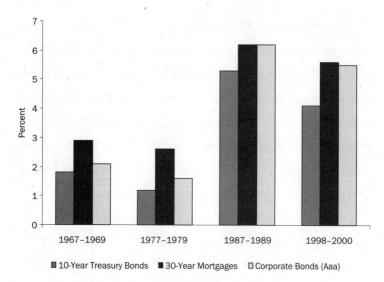

FIGURE 2.3 Real Interest Rates in the Clinton Boom
Source: Economic Report of the President.

was that the Clinton administration's policy of fueling a stock bubble and propping up the dollar were unsustainable. The stock-market bubble was inevitably going to burst, and the dollar couldn't remain overvalued indefinitely.

THE STOCK MARKET
AND SOCIAL SECURITY

There's little solid evidence, then, that the good economic news of the late 1990s can be traced to sound policy. In fact, the discussion of one major issue of that time shows how improvident U.S. policymakers had become.

In the new economy of the mid-1990s, Social Security was looking very old-fashioned. This quintessential New Deal social program had provided generations of workers with a certain level of economic security in their old age. It also provided protection against disability and support for families in the event of early death. Its administrative costs were extremely low (less than 0.6 percent of annual benefits), and corruption or fraud associated with the program was minimal. Essentially, the program did exactly what it was designed to do: provide enough income to workers and their families to allow them a basic standard of living in their retirement.

Conservative ideologues had long despised Social Security, but they knew it was very popular. Their best hope to eliminate Social Security lay in convincing the public that the program was in grave danger. Groups like the Concord Coalition, which was founded by Peter Peterson, an investment banker and Commerce Department secretary under Richard Nixon, argued that Social Security was on the edge of collapse. By the mid-1990s, a large portion of the public believed that Social Security needed a major overhaul to survive.

The program's savior seemed to be right in front of everyone's eyes. After all, the stock market could be counted on to rise year after year, or so it seemed. If it was possible to harness a portion of the market's phenomenal returns for individual retirement accounts in lieu of Social Security, every worker could be guaranteed a secure retirement. Proponents of Social Security privatization began circulating tracts promising that minimum wage workers would become millionaires under their plan.[6]

Even some of the experts grossly exaggerated the benefits of Social Security privatization. At the time, the standard assumption was that the stock market would provide an average real rate of return of 7 percent, a number extrapolated from past rates of return in the market. These projected rates were included in calculations made by many prominent economists and policy analysts, including those working at the Social Security Administration and the Congressional Budget Office (CBO).

There was one major problem with these calculations. Historically, the price-to-earnings ratio in the stock market had been much lower than it was in the mid-1990s. It was possible to sustain 7 percent real returns when the PE ratio was 14.5 to 1, but such returns couldn't be sustained when the PE ratio was over 20, as it was in the mid-1990s. It was certainly unsustainable when the PE ratio was over 30 to 1, as it was at the peaks of the bubble.[7]

To sustain those returns, the PE ratio would have to rise continuously, and at an accelerating rate. In a fairly short period of time, it would have to reach ratios of more than 50 to 1. Soon the PE ratio would cross 100 to 1. By the end of the 75-year Social Security projection period, the PE ratio would have to be several hundred to one, an implausible level. But in the heyday of the stock market bubble (and for many years afterward), policymakers believed the stock market was going to save Social Security, and they couldn't be bothered with arithmetic.

The push to fully or partially privatize Social Security received support from both parties in the mid-1990s. In fact, President Clinton was actively considering privatization plans at the end of 1997 and the beginning of 1998. As it turned out, these plans were derailed by the Monica Lewinsky scandal. When Clinton was impeached, he turned to traditional Democratic constituencies for support. And these constituencies—labor unions, African Americans, women's organizations, and others—were strongly committed to preserving Social Security in its current form.

The Lewinsky scandal was a remarkable historic event that came along fortuitously at just the moment when the Social Security program faced it greatest vulnerability. The Right had been largely successful in convincing the public that the program was on the edge of bankruptcy. Large segments of the public were convinced that the stock market was a perpetual-motion money machine, which provided an enormously promising alternative to Social Security's traditional form of finance: the payroll tax. And, there was a Democratic president who was willing to break with his party's longstanding support for the program in its current form. It is unlikely that there will be another set of circumstances that will place Social Security in as much danger.

CHAPTER 3

The Collapse of the Stock Bubble

As we saw in the previous chapter, the NASDAQ was the place to be in the 1990s. The New York Stock Exchange featured all the giants of the old economy, but the NASDAQ listed all the upstarts of the new economy, including Microsoft and Dell, as well as a vast array of technology and Internet companies that were being created in droves during this period.

A quick review of the NASDAQ numbers during that time reveals its startling growth. In 1995, the NASDAQ composite index was at 1000. It first crossed the 2000 threshold in December of 1998. By March 2000, it reached 5132, its all-time high. Its growth was rivaled only by its volatility. By the end of that year, the NASDAQ had closed at 2471, less than half its March peak (see figure 3.1), a decline that effectively wiped out all the gains since the beginning of 1999.

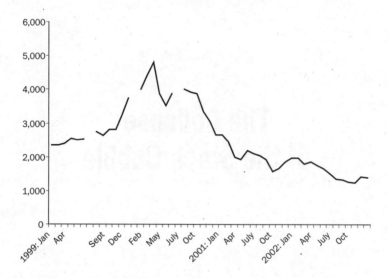

FIGURE 3.1 The NASDAQ Composite Index, 1999–2002

Source: Economic Report of the President, 2003.

But the slide wasn't over. The NASDAQ continued to fall through 2001 and finally bottomed out at 1108 in October of 2002, a level it hadn't seen since August 1996. In a span of two and a half years, the NASDAQ had lost 78.4 percent of its value, and the technology bubble had deflated.

Most of the start-up wonders of the new economy went down in flames. Many had started from scratch in the late 1990s, seen their stock prices rocket into the billions of dollars, then nosedived as quickly as they had soared. These companies included Webvan, a web-based grocer; Pets.com, an online pet supply store; and Flooz, a company that tried to establish a currency for online transactions.

This last company drew special notoriety because actress and comedian Whoopi Goldberg acted as its spokesperson. She agreed to be paid entirely in stock options for her work. Stock options were the main currency of this period; many workers agreed to accept them for the bulk of their compensation. When the boom collapsed, workers at many start-ups saw most of their value disappear. The television show *The Simpsons* captured the spirit of the tech bubble perfectly when it showed a start-up that dispensed options from a toilet paper roll.

The wreckage went far beyond ill-conceived start-ups. Established technology companies saw huge hits to their stock prices as well. Intel, the world's largest semiconductor company, had a market capitalization of almost $430 billion at its peak in the summer of 2000 before falling to $76 billion in October of 2002. Cisco, which designs and sells networking and communications technology, plummeted 89 percent from a market capitalization of over $470 billion to $51 billion between March of 2000 and October of 2002. Microsoft's capitalization dropped from more than $550 billion in December of 1999 to less than $200 billion in July of 2002.

The hit to the stock market went far beyond the technology sector. The S&P 500 index peaked at 1553 in March 2000, ended the year at 1320, and bottomed out in October 2002 at 769.

The cumulative loss in wealth from the peak of the market in 2000 to the trough in 2002 was close to $10 trillion, or $33,000 for every person in the country.

FALLOUT FROM THE CRASH: ACCOUNTING SCANDALS

The new economy, many observers felt at the time, called for new ways to measure company performance. During the boom years, the key accounting measure for most start-ups was EBITDA, which stood for "earnings before interest, taxes, depreciation and amortization." The markets focused on the quarterly releases of EBITDA, and many firms managed to meet or just exceed targets with remarkable regularity. This was enough to keep stockholders happy and share prices rising. But EBITDA wasn't a well-defined accounting concept, and companies had considerable leeway in how they measured it.

Once the market turned downward, investors became more interested in old-fashioned measures, such as profits and revenues. As it turned out, many firms weren't applying strict rules to these better-defined measures, either. For example, AOL had concocted an elaborate scheme with Homestore.com, an online real estate company. Through a complicated kickback process, AOL recorded extra revenue that made it look as if it was meeting growth targets.[1]

In the same vein, Global Crossing, a telecommunications company that started from scratch in 1997 and became a major national player by 2000, found a creative way to reach its financial targets. It engaged in regular swaps of capacity with Qwest, another major telecommunications company. However, the two companies booked the swaps differently, allowing Global Crossing to show a profit on the deals. The asymmetric treatment of the swaps occurred in spite of the fact that the same accounting firm, Arthur Anderson, was auditing the books of both companies.

But the shady dealings at AOL and Global Crossing were small change compared with WorldCom and Enron, two superstars of the new economy.

WorldCom was an amalgamation of telephone companies put together by Bernard Ebbers, an unorthodox Mississippi businessman. Ebbers started out in the telephone industry by forming a company in 1983 called Long Distance Discount Services, which purchased capacity in bulk from major carriers, such as AT&T, and resold the minutes at discount prices. The company, which soon changed its name to LDDS, went on a major acquisition spree over the next decade. After changing its name again to WorldCom in 1995, it acquired two telecom giants: MFS Communications in 1995 for $12 billion and MCI in 1997 for $40 billion. These acquisitions made WorldCom one of the largest communication companies in the world.

But Ebbers's management skills didn't match his flair for acquisitions. When it appeared that WorldCom would fail to meet profit projections in 1999, the company adopted creative accounting methods, depreciating capital equipment that should have been expensed. This allowed the company to understate its costs and, therefore, overstate profits. It also overstated revenue through improper accounting. WorldCom's auditor, Arthur Anderson, initially signed off on this accounting, although it did withdraw its audit after the fraud came to light in June 2002. When WorldCom filed for bankruptcy the following month, it became the largest company to do so in U.S. history.

In many ways, however, Enron's bankruptcy was an even more fitting final chapter to the new economy stock bubble. That company's story captures the spirit of the time and shows how supposedly levelheaded, clear-minded business people became caught up in the irrational exuberance of the late 1990s.

Enron was formed when two midsize natural gas companies merged in the mid-1980s. Under the leadership of Ken Lay, the merged company moved its headquarters from Omaha to

Houston and set about expanding into new lines of business. Its expansion was assisted by powerful political connections, including then Texas governor George W. Bush, who nicknamed Lay "Kenny Boy."

Enron moved quickly to take advantage of deregulation in the energy market, buying up companies and trading in energy and **derivative instruments.** It used its political connections to help further the process of deregulation and to take advantage of new opportunities. It also moved into buying and selling water and other products. In the bubble years, few economists or politicians questioned the wisdom of deregulating products like energy or water utilities, which had long been regulated as natural monopolies. Enron positioned itself to take advantage of this new way of thinking.

Enron also launched a public relations drive that secured it extraordinarily positive media coverage. It worked. *Fortune* magazine named Enron "America's Most Innovative Company" every year from 1996 to 2001. To help promote its image, Enron contributed to a long list of charitable and public interest groups, including environmental groups, some of which held it up as a model of a "green" energy company. Enron also offered a wide range of benefits to its workers, including paid family leave, which won it praise among those pushing for such benefits. Its management system, which was highlighted as a model for other companies to emulate, was touted as an "Idea Machine" in the *New York Times*.[2] Enron even bought ads at the Super Bowl in 1997, a rare move for a company that sells a commodity to utilities, given that the vast majority of the Superbowl audience is not among its potential customers.

Meanwhile, Enron kept expanding, reporting double-digit revenue and profit growth year after year. Its final profit binge was connected with the California energy crisis. The state had largely deregulated its electricity market during the 1990s, but in 2001, serious energy shortages sent electricity prices soaring. This meant much higher bills for families and businesses in areas where utility companies could pass along price increases to consumers. It meant nearly bankrupt providers where regulations prohibited passing on higher prices. In both cases, it meant soaring profits for Enron and some of the other big suppliers.

The Enron party ended in fall 2001, when its elaborate accounting fraud began to unravel. The real miracle of Enron, it turned out, lay in its creative bookkeeping. Enron hid billions of dollars of debt in its subsidiaries, allowing only the profits to show on its own books. Enron got away with its improper accounting because it had built up its reputation as a path-breaking innovator. It also had a willing accomplice in the Arthur Anderson accounting firm.

Enron quickly went from superstar to pariah. It sought bankruptcy protection in December 2001, and its top managers were subsequently indicted. Arthur Anderson, which was at the center of several major accounting scandals, also collapsed.

It was later discovered that Enron's profits in the California energy market involved a good deal more than pluck and luck. In yet another example of deregulation gone wrong, Enron exploited a recently deregulated and poorly designed energy market to create artificial shortages. The California electricity crisis produced skyrocketing energy prices and rolling blackouts, forcing Governor Gray Davis to declare a state of emergency. Forced to buy power at exorbitant rates, the state issued long-term debt obligations that deepened its budget crisis, and Governor Davis was subsequently recalled and replaced by Arnold Schwarzenegger. Enron's market manipulation earned the company another set of civil and criminal charges. In the course of the scandal, Ken Lay even lost his nickname from President Bush, who began to refer to him as "Mr. Lay."

Enron's fraudulent practices were exposed in 2001, marking the end of the era of irrational exuberance. Investors began to take accounting very seriously. In July 2002, Congress passed the Sarbanes-Oxley Act, which imposed tighter rules on corporate accounting.

But the new law didn't address the fundamental conflict at the center of the Enron-era accounting scandals: the fact that companies picked their own auditors. Even though auditors were supposed to apply accounting rules objectively and disinterestedly, the risk of losing major clients gave them an incentive to accept questionable accounting practices.

This problem could have been easily addressed by taking the selection of an auditor out of the hands of the company being audited. One way to do this would be to have the stock exchange where a company is listed assign auditors randomly. Companies could then be allowed to refuse or replace auditors but only by presenting a public complaint. Even then, the company could be denied the chance to pick the replacement auditor. However, Congress chose not to adopt such measures that would have eliminated this fundamental conflict of interest.

Sarbanes-Oxley also failed to address one of the other accounting abuses of this period. In the early 1990s, Senator Joe Lieberman led an effort to prevent the Financial Accounting Standards Board (FASB) from requiring the expensing of stock options. As a result of Senator Lieberman's effort, companies could pass out as many options as they chose and effectively list them on their books as having zero cost. This led to an enormous overstatement of profits for technology startups that depended heavily on options to cover labor and other expenses.

FURTHER FALLOUT
FROM THE STOCK BUBBLE

If accounting scandals were one subplot of the stock-bubble story, another was misdirected investment. Soaring stock prices made it easy for many high-tech entrepreneurs to raise capital, but many of these companies had no serious prospects of success. Meanwhile, manufacturing companies had more and more difficulty acquiring capital to refurbish their plants and thus compete more effectively in international markets.

In addition to steering capital away from these firms, the stock bubble also hurt the manufacturing sector by further inflating the dollar. Hundreds of billions of dollars flowed in from foreign investors who wanted to get in on the NASDAQ's race to the sky. This huge inflow supported the high dollar at the end of the 1990s. The high dollar, in turn, made U.S. manufacturers less competitive internationally.

The collapse of the stock bubble then led to a pension crisis. Most companies with **defined-benefit pension plans** contributed little or nothing to these plans during the bubble years, when the stock market rose enough to meet required funding levels. But when stocks tumbled, many of the country's largest pension funds became hugely underfunded, creating a shortfall that threatened the financial stability of otherwise healthy companies. Again, the manufacturing sector, where defined-benefit pensions are concentrated, was hit the hardest. Several large companies, most notably in the steel industry, declared bankruptcy and turned over their underfunded pension plans to the Pension Benefit Guarantee Corporation (PBGC), a federal corporation that protects the pensions of nearly 44 million Americans.

The airline industry also had many defined-benefit pension plans that were badly underfunded. Still reeling from the 2001 recession and the decline in air traffic following the September 2001 attacks, the airlines were poorly situated to make up the shortfall. Two major airlines, Pan Am and TWA, went out of business and turned over their underfunded pensions to the PBGC. Several other airlines, including United, Delta, and US Air, subsequently declared bankruptcy and passed along much of their pension obligations to the PBGC. As a result of these bankruptcies, the PBGC is likely to face substantial financing problems itself in coming years.

Probably the most serious fallout from the stock bubble was then and remains now less obvious than these high-profile failures. With the market rising at double-digit rates through the second half of the 1990s, many workers saw little reason to save for their retirement from their current income. Just when baby boomers were entering what should have been their peak savings years, saving as a share of disposable income hit the lowest levels ever seen. The saving rate averaged 9 percent in the 1980s. It fell to just 2.3 percent in 2000.[3]

THE ECONOMISTS GET IT WRONG

Virtually no economists or analysts expected the stock market crash and the resulting recession. In the fall of 2000, not one of the 50 most prominent "Blue Chip" forecasters saw a recession coming the following year. In fact, the lowest growth projection for 2001 among them was 2.2 percent.

The same was true of the 31 eminent forecasters surveyed by the Federal Reserve Bank of Philadelphia for its Livingston Survey in December 2000. The group saw nothing but blue skies ahead. It expected the stock market to recover the losses it had suffered over the year and rise to new heights in the year ahead (see table 3.1).

The Congressional Budget Office (CBO) was also among those surprised by the downturn and the collapse of the stock bubble. The CBO outlook had been rosy, projecting real GDP growth for the year of 2.4 percent in the "Budget and Economic Outlook" that it publishes each January. That faulty prediction caused CBO to hugely overestimate capital gains tax revenue by almost $70 billion more than had been projected in both 2002 and 2003. This estimation error was a major factor leading to the large increase in the budget deficit in these years.

TABLE 3.1 Livingston Survey, December 2000, and Actual Outcomes

	Median Forecast	Actual
Unemployment 2001	4.3%	4.8%
Unemployment 2002	4.5%	5.8%
GDP Growth 2001	3.1%	0.8%
GDP Growth 2002	3.5%	1.9%
S&P 500 2001 (end)	1490	1148
S&P 500 2002 (end)	1639.5	880

Source: Federal Reserve Bank of Philadelphia.

In retrospect, much of the budget policy debate at the time looks silly. (To some of us, it looked pretty silly at the time.) Candidates running for office took for granted the CBO budget projections and then argued over what year we should target for paying off the national debt. Some thought we could do it by 2008, and others suggested that 2013 was a better goal.

Naturally, Alan Greenspan got into the act. He wondered how the Fed would conduct monetary policy when there was no government debt for the Fed to purchase. (The Fed conducts its monetary policy by buying and selling government debt.) At one point, the Fed's researchers considered the possibility of using **mortgage-backed securities** as a tool to conduct monetary policy.

The issue of eliminating government debt figured in Greenspan's support for President Bush's tax cuts. In January of 2001, Greenspan told Congress, "Indeed, in almost any credible baseline scenario, short of a major and prolonged economic contraction, the full benefits of debt reduction are now achieved before the end of this decade."[4] This was Greenspan's way of saying that he thought the national debt would be paid off by 2010. The government would then have to use its surplus to buy private assets, a route that Greenspan opposed. He therefore endorsed tax cuts to slow the rate at which the debt would be paid off.

When the economy sank into recession less than two months later, Greenspan found relief from his fears that the government would pay off its debt too quickly. The revenue loss associated with the recession, coupled with the loss of capital gains tax revenue in the wake of the stock crash, would have pushed the budget into deficit in any case. But President Bush's tax cuts increased the size of the deficit, as did the spending associated with the war in Afghanistan and later Iraq.

As is standard practice in Washington policy circles, few experts suffered any serious consequences for failing to recognize the stock bubble or the risks it entailed. It was common to pretend as though the bubble had been widely recognized

(continued on page 60)

How to Recognize a Stock Bubble

Recognizing a stock market bubble requires only a little bit of arithmetic. The key is the price-to-earnings (PE) ratio in the stock market. Historically, this ratio has been close to 15 to 1. At this ratio, if companies pay out 50 to 60 percent of their profits as dividends (roughly the historic average), shareholders will receive dividend yields of between 3.3 percent and 4 percent.[5]

If the economy grows by 3 to 3.5 percent annually (adjusted for inflation), and the PE ratio remains constant, stock prices will rise by the same amount. This gives a total inflation-adjusted return of between 6.3 percent and 7.5 percent, the range seen between the end of the depression and the run-up in share prices in the late 1990s.

That run-up wasn't accompanied by a corresponding increase in corporate profits, which meant that the market as a whole had a large increase in the PE ratio. At its peak value in March of 2000, the PE ratio exceeded 30.

This record value indicates a stock bubble. If the PE ratio is 30 and corporations pay out 50 to 60 percent of their profits as dividends, the dividend payout is equal to just 1.6 to 2 percent of the share price. Furthermore, with labor force growth slowing as a result of the baby-boom cohort leaving the workforce, GDP growth was projected to slow to less than 3 percent a year. This meant that capital gains would average 3 percent or less.

If the dividend yield is between 1.6 and 2 percent of the share price, and the capital gain averages less than 3 percent annually, the expected real return on stock would be between 4.6 and 5 percent annually, far below the historic average. But for stocks to provide their historic 7 percent real rate of return, firms would have to pay out all of their profits in dividends. This scenario is implausible because firms would have no money left to reinvest in their operations.

Alternatively, stock prices could rise more rapidly than the growth in corporate profits. However, this phenomenon would increase the PE ratio. If that ratio continues to rise, we fairly quickly reach ratios that seem implausible. Unless shareholders are willing to hold stocks for returns that are far lower than they had historically demanded, the record PE ratios of the late 1990s could only be the result of a speculative bubble.

It should have been a simple matter in the late 1990s to see that the stock market had entered a bubble. It was necessary to believe that either shareholders were suddenly willing to accept very low returns on their stock or that the economy was going to grow much faster than all the experts thought it would. Certainly the vast majority of stock enthusiasts among the money managers had no qualitatively different assessment of the economy's prospects than most of the leading economic forecasters. In other words, they had no reason to believe that the stock market would generate the sort of returns that they were promising to clients.

and its collapse unsurprising. The fact that most experts didn't recognize the bubble at all was politely ignored.

Greenspan stands out in this respect. He later told audiences that he had recognized the stock bubble but decided to let it run its course and deal with the fallout. The Fed's meeting transcripts show that Greenspan did, in fact, recognize the bubble early on, but the fallout proved to be more vexing than he may have imagined.

More troublesome, perhaps, is the fact that this understanding of the stock bubble was inconsistent with Greenspan's testimony in favor of the Bush tax cuts. If Greenspan recognized the bubble, then he knew it would collapse. This collapse would almost certainly cause a recession and lead to a sharp falloff in capital gains tax revenue. In that case, Greenspan should have known that his concern about the country paying off its debt too quickly was unfounded. The conclusion is inescapable: if Greenspan foresaw the bubble, his stated reason for supporting President Bush's tax cuts couldn't have been his real motive.

THE RECESSION HITS

The collapse of the stock market bubble led to the first investment-led recession of the postwar period. Nominal investment—versus real investment, which takes into account the rate of inflation—fell by more than $50 billion from 2000 to 2001, leading to a decline of a full percentage point in the investment share of GDP. Earlier recessions had been driven by drops in home building and car purchases due to rising interest rates.

This distinction is important because it's easier to recover from this more traditional form of recession. To fix that problem, the Fed can simply lower interest rates. This sets the process in reverse by boosting car purchases, home sales, and construction. This upturn is often steep. Recessions can create pent-up demand because families put off buying cars or homes. By lowering interest rates, the Fed can release that pent-up demand.

It's much harder to stimulate the economy when the recession is the result of a downturn in investment. Even sharp declines in interest rates are likely to have only a minimal impact on investment. In 2001 and 2002, there wasn't a large pent-up demand in the housing or auto sector. This meant that lower interest rates would have only a very limited demand on growth.

Nevertheless, the Fed lowered interest rates aggressively during this period, dropping the federal funds rate down from 6.5 percent in December 2000 to 3.75 percent in the summer of 2001. After the attacks of September 11, 2001, the Fed responded with even more rate cuts, pushing the rate down to

1.75 percent by the end of the year. The rate bottomed out at 1 percent in summer 2003. The Fed held that rate, the lowest in almost half a century, for a full year.

Meanwhile, the economy began to shed jobs in March 2001 and continued to do so into 2003. The economy didn't begin to add jobs consistently until September of 2003, and it didn't regain the jobs lost in the downturn until February 2005. The weaker labor market had the predictable effect on wage growth, which didn't return until 2006.

FISCAL POLICY AND THE DOLLAR

The sharp falloff in investment required an effective response from the federal government. In fact, the government did boost the economy in 2001, even if its action wasn't deliberately designed to counteract the recession.

In his 2000 presidential campaign, President Bush promised lower taxes. Specifically, he proposed a 15 percent across-the-board cut in income tax rates, which would reduce revenue by approximately $150 billion a year. At the time, the government was running large surpluses and was projected to do so long into the future. When President Bush first requested the tax cut from Congress, he argued that the large surplus showed that the American people were overpaying, and he was there to ask for a refund.

As the economy slumped in 2001, the rationale for the tax cut changed. It suddenly became an insurance policy against a recession. This claim was made more credible by sending a $300 rebate check to the vast majority of taxpayers. The Bush tax cut undoubtedly boosted the economy in 2001 and 2002. The rebate checks in particular proved to be especially timely, given the fallout from attacks of September 2001. Of course, Congress had no idea those attacks were forthcoming when it passed its tax cut.

A large percentage of these rebate checks was spent quickly, which kept the economy from sinking further. It would have been easy, however, to design more effective ways to boost the economy. If Congress had devoted the same funds to promoting infrastructure projects, education, clean energy, or conservation, the stimulatory impact would have been greater and longer lasting. It would also have been simple to design more effective tax cuts for that same purpose. If more of the benefits went to taxpayers at the middle or bottom of the income distribution, rather than to those at the top, the tax cut would have been even more helpful. It's unlikely that the tax cut led Bill Gates to increase his consumption in any noticeable way.

But these policies could address only part of the problem. The biggest imbalance facing the economy at the time was the large trade deficit, which stood at almost $370 billion in 2001, approximately 3.6 percent of GDP. The country was import-

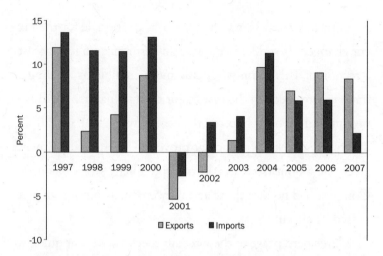

FIGURE 3.2 Growth in Real Exports and Imports, 1997–2007

Source: Bureau of Economic Analysis, National Income and Product Accounts.

ing much more than it was exporting due to the overvalued dollar. Typically, when the economy goes into a recession, the downward trajectory is partly offset by an improvement on the trade balance. The slowing economy reduces the domestic demand for everything, including imports, so we expect to see the country's trade balance improve during a downturn.

The opposite happened in the 2001 recession and the periods of weak growth that followed. In fact, the trade deficit continued to expand (see figure 3.2). Imports grew at a rapid pace every year during this period with the exception of 2001 recession year, when there was a modest drop in imports.

However, the drop in exports in 2001 was considerably larger. Because exports fell even more than imports through this period of economic weakness, the trade deficit continued to grow. This placed a further drag on the economy rather than providing the expected countercyclical effect.

The reason for the perverse movement in the trade balance was that investors and foreign central banks were eager to hold dollar assets, even as interest rates in the United States sank to 50-year lows. The rationale of the central banks is perhaps the most easily explained. Major exporting countries, most importantly China, wanted to keep the value of their currencies low relative to the dollar. In part, this desire was a response to an earlier financial crisis that led to International Monetary Fund (IMF) restrictions on many East Asian countries. Reluctant to deal with the IMF again, central banks in Asia stockpiled dollars and kept their own currencies undervalued. This reaction put downward pressure on the U.S. price of Asian products and upward pressure on the trade deficit.

Central banks in Asia were virtually certain to take large losses when they bought overvalued dollars and held Treasury bonds that paid miniscule returns. Even so, these countries maintained their export markets during these years. Whether or not this was a shrewd strategy for these countries is debatable; certainly China's extraordinary growth during this time suggests that its policy wasn't too harmful. In any case, the

overvalued dollar made it more difficult for the United States
to recover from the stock crash. The trade deficit continued
to expand throughout this period, peaking at 5.7 percent of
GDP in 2006.

The correct policy at the time would have been to push the
dollar down—for example, by selling dollars in international
currency markets—in order to bring the trade deficit back to
a manageable level. But that policy would have had undesirable short-term effects, most notably higher import prices.
As far as its impact on U.S. living standards, a lower dollar is
comparable to a tax increase. Just as few politicians push for
tax increases, regardless of how badly they may be needed, few
politicians are eager to call for a lower dollar.

Neither the Treasury nor the Fed expressed any interest in
this option. Instead, the country hitched its wagon to the next
financial bubble.

CHAPTER 4

The Beginnings of the Housing Bubble

At the end of 1996, my future wife and I decided to move in together in Washington, DC. We saw an advertisement for a two-bedroom apartment in a neighborhood we both liked. It rented for $1,600 a month. But when we saw it, we discovered that it was a basement apartment, which neither of us wanted.

We both had some savings, so we decided to look into buying a condominium in the area. We quickly found one we liked and purchased it for $160,000. With a 20-percent down payment and a 30-year fixed rate mortgage at 7 percent, our monthly payment was under $900. Fees and taxes raised that to $1,350 a month. This was $250 less than we would have paid for renting the basement apartment on the next block, even before taking into account the tax deductions on the interest and property tax. Owning seemed like a good decision.

At that time, the DC area was coming out of a housing slump, which no doubt affected these numbers. But in most areas around the country at that time, there was a close relationship between the cost of renting and owning comparable units. This relationship broke down during the housing bubble years. House prices soared, doubling or even tripling in the most bubble-inflated markets. Yet, no major metropolitan area saw the same double-digit increases in rental prices as they did in sale prices. This led to a huge gap between ownership costs and rental costs.

My wife and I decided to sell our condominium in 2004, seven years after we had purchased it. Apart from painting it, we had put virtually no money into repairs or renovations. Within two weeks, the unit sold for $445,000. This was an increase of 178 percent from the price we paid. Even after adjusting for inflation, the gain was still 158 percent.

We went back to renting and found a similar apartment in the same neighborhood for $2,200 a month. The sale price of the condo had risen 178 percent, but our new apartment rented for just 37.5 percent more than the basement unit in 1996. The housing bubble had radically altered the economics of owning and renting.

THE PROPHETS OF BOOM

At the peak of the housing bubble in 2005, David Lereah, the chief economist of the National Association of Realtors, published his classic book, *Why the Real Estate Boom Will Not Bust and How You Can Profit from It*. At the time, Mr. Lereah was by far the most widely quoted authority on the housing market. His views regularly appeared in the *Wall Street Journal*, the *Washington Post*, and hundreds of other news outlets across the country.

Somehow, it never occurred to reporters that the chief economist of the National Association of Realtors was in the business of selling real estate. Otherwise, they might have viewed his predictions of ever-rising house prices a bit more skeptically. Even better, they might have balanced those predictions with the views of experts holding different opinions. Very little skepticism about the housing boom was voiced in news reporting in 2005, or indeed until the bubble began to collapse under its own weight the following year.

In fairness to the media, few economists offered critical assessments of the housing market. Only a few years earlier, virtually the entire economics profession managed to miss the $10 trillion stock bubble. Now it was the rare economist who noted anything unusual about housing prices, even though they were completely inconsistent with past trends or current rents and income.

Once again, the boom-time intoxication set in. As long as house prices kept rising, there was little need to ask questions. In Los Angeles, the average price of a home rose from $161,000 in 1995 to $228,000 in 2000.[1] It then soared to $585,000 in 2006. But everyone knows that Los Angeles has a great climate and a rapidly growing entertainment industry.

Tampa also has a great climate. With tens of millions of baby boomers retiring over the next two decades, Tampa would be inundated with snowbirds. The average price of a home in Tampa rose from $84,000 in 1995 to $102,000 in 2000. It then spiked to $229,000 in 2006. Tampa enthusiasts noted that their prices were still low compared to those of other metropolitan areas, including Miami's, where house prices rose by 218 percent from 1995 to 2006. Phoenix also experienced a boom. The average price of a house there rose from $92,000 in 1995 to $124,000 in 2000 before peaking at $268,000 in 2006. This was an increase of 192 percent in one decade.

But prices weren't rising only in the Sun Belt. In Seattle, the average house price rose from 145 percent between 1995 and 2006, increasing from $147,000 to $361,000. This was explained by the fact that Seattle was a clean, vibrant city surrounded by mountains and Puget Sound. Also, thanks to

Microsoft, Seattle was at the center of software development for the whole world.

San Francisco saw the average price of a home increase from $234,000 in 1995 to $753,000 in 2006, a rise of 221 percent. San Francisco is one of the most beautiful cities of the world, dominated by streets lined with charming homes built in the early years of the last century.

After some tough years in the 1970s and 1980s, Chicago was revitalized in the 1990s. The average price of a house in Chicago rose from $136,000 in 1995 to $274,000 in 2006, an increase of 101 percent.

Property values in New York and Boston had long ranked near the top in the country, but that didn't mean they couldn't go higher. The price of an average home in Boston rose from $159,000 in 1995 to $402,000 in 2006, an increase of 153 percent. In New York, the average house price rose by 173 percent, from $172,000 in 1995 to $469,000 in 2006. Boston has enormous charm and history, plus a vibrant economy resulting from the spin-offs and start-ups emerging from research and development in the area. As a major cultural and financial center, New York was creating many high-paying jobs.

And so the stories went. Wherever house prices went through the roof, residents and realtors explained the trend in terms of their city's unique appeal. After all, there's only one Miami, Tampa, Phoenix, San Francisco, Los Angeles, Seattle,

Chicago, Washington DC, New York, and Boston. And, whatever else happened in the economy, homeowners in these cities were confident that their investments were safe.

THE LOGIC
OF THE HOUSING BUBBLE

Financial bubbles grow from their own momentum. In the case of the housing bubble, the story was straightforward. Homeowners in some regions saw the value of their homes double or even triple in very short periods of time. Because houses are highly leveraged—buyers typically pay a small fraction of the house price and borrow the rest—it's relatively easy to become very rich by buying and selling them in a rising market. A homeowner who put down $10,000 on a $200,000 home and saw its price double could pocket $200,000. Soaring house prices made every homeowner a brilliant investor.

As prices rose year after year, homeowners came to view rapid appreciation as the natural order of things, and home-buyers began to view prices differently. A $400,000 home looks much more affordable if it's likely to sell for $500,000 just a few years down the road. In this way, expectations of rising house prices become self-fulfilling. The expectation of higher house prices in the future means buyers will pay more today. This willingness, in turn, causes prices to rise.

Buying a house is much easier than starting a business, and many middle-class families have come to view houses as investments as well as shelter. Sometimes this view means keeping a house as an investment property after moving to a new home. In other cases, it means seeking out properties to hold and sell with the expectation of turning a profit. The soaring house prices of the bubble years encouraged both types of behavior. Millions of middle-class families came to own multiple homes in these years as a way to cash in on the housing boom. This was yet another factor pushing house prices higher. Investors were prepared to snap up new homes quickly with the expectation that they could sell them for a higher price in the near future. In 2004, more than a quarter of homes sold were bought as investments, according to the National Association of Realtors.

Newspapers were filled with stories of buyers flipping houses or condominiums for huge profits. For example, the *Washington Post* told of an investor who made a profit of $153,000 by buying and selling a condo within the same day.[2] Another article told of a waiter who lived in a $500,000 condominium and rented out a second one. "Real estate is never going to be worth nothing," the waiter said. "It's not some tech-bubble stock."[3] There were comparable media stories in bubble markets across the country.

How does this kind of upward spiral get started? In the United States, the origins of the housing bubble can be found in the stock bubble and its collapse. When stock prices rose, stockholders used their wealth to buy things, including houses. Because the supply of housing is relatively fixed in the short term, the increased demand put upward pressure on house prices. In this way, flight from the volatile stock market helped create a new bubble.

In the 1980s, a similar development unfolded in Japan, but the two bubbles were more intertwined there. Investors borrowed against their real estate to buy stock and vice versa. The bubbles also grew much larger in Japan relative to the size of its economy. For example, Japan's stock-bubble market was valued at more than $8 trillion at its peak in 1990, almost four times the size of Japan's economy. The U.S. stock bubble peaked in early 2000 at just over twice the size of the U.S. economy.

Japan's stock and real-estate bubble burst more or less simultaneously in 1990. This collapse threw the Japanese economy into a slump from which it still hasn't fully recovered. During its bubble years, Japan's economy was envied around the world. Economists analyzed its institutions in an effort to increase growth rates in the United States, Europe, and elsewhere. To many it seemed only a matter of time before Japan displaced the United States as the world's preeminent economic power. This situation changed quickly after the collapse of the bubbles. Instead of Japan being presented as a model to be followed, it was a mistake to be avoided. In the end, however, the lesson was lost on American investors and policymakers.

THE BUBBLE DENIERS

The stock market collapse fueled the housing bubble in two ways. First, there was the simple response by investors who had been burned in the stock crash. Even though these investors were willing to believe outlandish claims about stock prices in the late 1990s, many became wary of the stock market's volatility. Besides, housing was tangible wealth. "You can always live in your house," investors told one another.

The second way the stock market crash fueled the housing bubble was indirect. After the crash, the Federal Reserve Board pushed interest rates down to their lowest point in almost 50 years. These low interest rates helped to sustain rising prices in a housing market that was already seriously overvalued.

Eager to foster growth however he could, Alan Greenspan tried to preempt talk of irrational exuberance in the housing market. In 2002, he testified before Congress that there was no bubble.[4] When I read that testimony at the time, however, I noticed that none of his arguments made any sense. I decided to examine the evidence and soon concluded that there was indeed a bubble in the housing market.[5]

Even as early as 2002, Greenspan's argument was a tough

one to make. At the time, it was easy to use government data to show that house prices had tracked the overall rate of inflation from 1953 to 1995.[6] (A couple of years later, Yale professor Robert Shiller found that the same pattern stretched back to 1895.) But between 1995 and 2006, house prices rose by more than 70 percent, even after adjusting for inflation. In the absence of any big changes in the supply and demand of housing, a price bubble seemed to be the only rational explanation.

In his 2002 congressional testimony, however, Greenspan cited four factors that supposedly provided a fundamental basis for the run-up in house prices: shortages of land, environmental restrictions on buildings, growing incomes, and a growing population. None, however, provided a plausible basis for the kinds of price increases we were seeing during those years.

Let's look at those factors one at a time. There's no obvious reason why the limited supply of land would have suddenly pushed up house prices for the nation as a whole in 1995. In fact, new opportunities for telecommuting offered by the Internet should have alleviated pressures arising from land shortages. In the late 1990s, prophets of the new economy were fond of claiming that restrictions of space and time no longer mattered. Even though such statements were often far-fetched, they had a grain of truth. The Internet should have reduced the premium that buyers were willing to pay to live in desirable locations.

The second claim, that environmental restrictions made it more difficult to build new housing, also suffered from a timing problem. There had been serious environmental restrictions on building in much of the country since at least the 1960s, but there was no reason to believe that they became tighter in the late 1990s. In fact, antienvironmental conservatives were well represented at all levels of government, and the pace of construction was beginning to approach record levels.

If nothing on the supply side could explain the run-up in house prices, the arguments on the demand side were no more plausible. Income grew at a healthy pace from 1996 to 2001, but that growth was quite weak during and after the 2001 recession. If the extraordinary income growth following World War II didn't lead to an increase in real house prices, the mediocre income growth between 1996 and 2006 surely couldn't explain such dramatic run-ups to inflation-adjusted prices.

Similarly, population growth was slowing during these years. The baby boomers had long since entered the workforce and established their households. The age cohorts that followed were considerably smaller, hence the alarm over Social Security. If demographics was the cause of the run-up in house prices, there should have been a much larger run-up in the

1970s and 1980s, when the baby boomers were first forming their own households.

In short, none of Greenspan's four factors came close to explaining the economic reality on the ground. In the absence of obvious smoking guns—and anything that drives up prices so dramatically would be hard to miss—it took no special insight to conclude that the run-up reflected a price bubble that would, at some point, deflate.

Big-picture explanations aside, there's another easy way to check for the presence of a housing price bubble, and we saw it at the beginning of this chapter: we can compare house prices with rents. If market fundamentals are responsible for an increase in sale prices, the same factors should also be putting upward pressure on rents. But rents didn't rise substantially faster than inflation through most of this period, and they rose at the same rate or even slightly below the rate of inflation in the years after 2002. This should have been a clear warning to the experts, and the public, about the future direction in house prices.

One other fundamental factor—low interest rates—has also been offered as a reason for rapidly rising house prices during this period. If buyers are concerned only about their monthly mortgage payments, a low interest rate can push up house prices. But rather than contradicting the bubble view, this argument actually supports it. If low interest rates were the main factor that explained high house prices, the return of interest rates to normal levels would send house prices plunging back to their **trend levels.**

In effect, this argument implied that house prices had entered a new era of unprecedented volatility. If buyers purchase homes when interest rates are very low, they risk losses when higher rates push down the value of their homes. On the other hand, those who buy when interest rates are very high may experience large gains if interest rates subsequently decline. House prices have not historically been that sensitive to interest rates, but if low interest rates explained the run-up in house prices, this explanation meant that the country had entered a new era in which house prices could fluctuate dramatically over the course of a business cycle. This account of the housing market was consistent with the bubble view and implies that homeownership in the future would be a far riskier proposition than it had been in the past.

If economists and analysts still weren't convinced that a housing bubble existed, there was one other way to check. They could have looked at the Census Bureau's data on vacancy rates, which indicates how tight or loose the housing market is. During the early years of the bubble, in fact, the vacancy rate on rental units rose rapidly (see figure 4.1).

The vacancy rate on ownership units stood at 1.6 percent in 1996, before the bubble really took hold. It started rising rap-

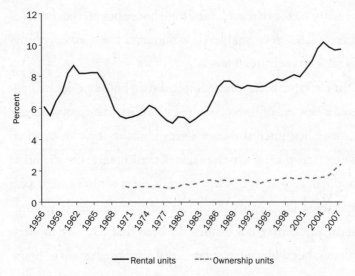

FIGURE 4.1 Vacancy Rates: Rental and Ownership Units
Source: Census Bureau.

idly in 2005 and averaged 2.4 percent for 2007. Even though an increase from 1.6 percent to 2.4 percent may seem of little consequence, the 2007 vacancy rate was 50 percent higher than it was at any prior point in the postwar period.

It's difficult to reconcile a rising vacancy rate, which almost by definition means excess supply, with a housing shortage. Presumably the increase in rental vacancies reflected the decision of many renters to become homeowners, leaving their landlords with empty units. However, it was absurd to imagine that an excess supply of rental units would have no effect on sale prices. Eventually landlords would drop rents on vacant units by amounts large enough to pull people away from owning.

Although Greenspan had no valid grounds for his claims, he frequently repeated his contention that there was no bubble and therefore no reason to be concerned about a potential crash. He also dismissed calls, including those from his fellow Federal Reserve Board governor Edward Gramlich, to examine the questionable lending practices that became more and more widespread as the bubble grew larger.

In late 2003, Greenspan defied logic again by suggesting that homeowners take out **adjustable-rate mortgages (ARMs)**. At the time, the 30-year mortgage rate was near a 50-year low. Greenspan later claimed that he was merely commenting on recent research that showed that many homeowners would have saved money with such mortgages. But he almost certainly knew that his comments were being reported and passed along as an endorsement of ARMs. If Greenspan believed that his comments had been misrepresented, he had ample opportunity to set the record straight with an explicit statement or press release. His failure to do so indicates that he wasn't concerned about the effect his comment may have had in promoting those mortgages at such an inopportune time.

In 2004, the Federal Reserve published a research paper that supported Greenspan's public testimony about the absence of a housing bubble and that sought to undermine the case for such a bubble. The paper, which received a great deal of attention, was coauthored by Jonathan McCarthy and Richard Peach, the vice president of the New York Federal Reserve Bank.[7] It argued that the federal House Price Index (HPI) substantially overstated the true rate of increase in house prices because it failed to include improvements in the houses that appeared in the index.

The HPI was widely viewed as a good measure of the change in house prices. Because it tracked resales of the same houses, it wasn't affected by changes in the mix of homes in the sample. By contrast, other measures could be misleading if relatively more high-end or low-end homes were sold in a given month. McCarthy and Peach argued that the main reason that the HPI had risen so rapidly in the years since 1995 was that the homes in the sample were being improved rapidly. They recommended an alternative measure from the Census Bureau, which measured the cost of construction through time but didn't pick up increases in land values. This data showed no comparable increase in house prices. In fact, the Census Bureau's series increased only slightly more rapidly than the overall rate of inflation through this period.

There was an easy way to test the plausibility of McCarthy and Peach's claim. The Census Bureau also collected data on repairs and renovations. If it was true that the more rapid run-up in house prices was driven by improvements, that data should have reflected a large increase in spending on such improvements during this period. The opposite, however, was true. Spending on improvements actually fell relative to house values during this period.[8] Furthermore, the order of magnitude in McCarthy and Peach's paper was clearly faulty. Spending on house repairs and improvements was close to $100 billion a year, but the value of existing homes was rising at the rate of close to $1 trillion a year. The claim that $100 billion spent on improvements could increase house values by $1 trillion wouldn't ordinarily pass the laugh test among economists. But in the heyday of the housing bubble, the vice president of the New York Federal Reserve Board was willing to publish that claim in a research paper.

The contingent of bubble promoters went well beyond the Fed. Eager to tout the virtues of homeownership, economists at Fannie Mae and Freddie Mac insisted that warnings of a housing bubble were ridiculous. Frank Nothaft, the chief economist at Freddie Mac, repeatedly told audiences that nationwide house prices never fall. The economists and spokespeople for the National Association of Homebuilders, the Mortgage Bankers Association, and the National Association of Realtors pushed homeownership even as the bubble expanded to ever more dangerous levels.

Remarkably, the media unquestioningly passed along those

views to the public as if representatives of industry groups were impartial analysts. These views were almost never challenged by disinterested economists offering a qualitatively different assessment of the housing market. Only in the winter of 2007, when the meltdown was well under way, did a few economists note anything unusual. Even then, the vast majority of economists minimized the extent of the problem, dismissing the idea that the collapse of the housing market would lead to a recession and a financial crisis.

THE OWNERSHIP SOCIETY

Another factor driving house prices up was the push to turn less wealthy families into homeowners. The government has long promoted homeownership through a wide range of policies, such as the tax deduction for mortgage interest and the exemption of most capital gains on housing from taxation. However, the push for homeownership became even more of an ideological crusade during the bubble years. Programs to assist low-income renters were cut, while new money was made available to promote homeownership.

Among the items in the latter category was President Bush's "American Dream" fund, which provided down-payment assistance to low-income families. With President Bush's encouragement, the private sector joined the crusade. Financial institutions, including the huge government-created mortgage giants, Fannie Mae and Freddie Mac, did their part by buying up hundreds of billions of dollars of subprime and Alt-A mortgages contained in mortgage-backed securities. (Alt-A mortgages are issued to homebuyers who have better credit scores than subprime buyers but are still ineligible for prime mortgages.) It's important to note that Fannie and Freddie followed the private sector in this area. In fact, they lost market share to private-sector issuers during the peak bubble years.

Many private foundations and charities also helped low-income families become homeowners. Instead of focusing on increasing the incomes of these families, they promoted "asset building," with homeownership being a big part of the story.

The promotion of homeownership during these years was successful. The overall homeownership rate rose from 64 percent in 1994 to a peak of 69 percent in 2004 (figure 4.2). Some of this increase was attributable to demographics. As people age, they're far more likely to be homeowners, and with the baby boomers passing into middle age, there was good reason to expect some increase in homeownership in any case. However, the rise in homeownership during these years far exceeds what could be explained by the aging of the population.

This push toward homeownership helped inflate the bubble because it created more potential buyers. It also helped the bubble deniers and undermined the efforts of those who were

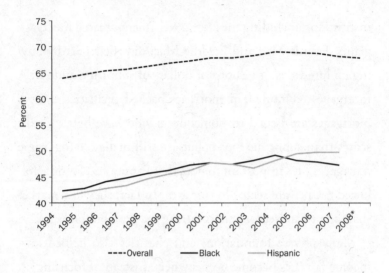

FIGURE 4.2 Homeownership Rates during the Boom

*2008 data for first half of year only

Source: Census Bureau.

calling attention to risks in the housing market. The promoters of homeownership insisted that everything was fine and encouraged potential homebuyers and reporters to ignore those who were warning about the overvaluation of house prices.

The increase in homeownership rates for African American and Latino families was especially dramatic. The homeownership rate for African Americans rose from 42.3 percent in 1994 to 49.1 percent in 2004. The homeownership rate for Latinos rose from 41.2 percent in 1994 to 49.7 in 2008.

Part of these increases proved to be temporary. Since its

peak in 2004, the homeownership rate for African Americans fell by 1.6 percentage points to 47.5 percent in the first half of 2008. This rate is the same as the rate of homeownership among African Americans in 2000, before most of the boom. Similarly, the rate of homeownership for Latinos has drifted down slightly to 49.3 percent in the wake of the subprime crisis. The overall homeownership rate fell by one percentage point, from its peak of 69 percent in 2004 to 68 percent in 2008. This rate is the same as the rate the country had in 2002. With foreclosures still on the rise, it is virtually certain that homeownership rates will continue to decline in the next year and a half, reversing more of the gains in homeownership for African Americans, Latinos, and the country as a whole.

FUN WITH THE HOUSING BUBBLE

With house prices going through the roof, home equity became an important source of wealth for millions of families. Many took out home equity loans or new mortgages that were larger than existing mortgages in order to buy cars and boats, take vacations, or pay bills. Savings out of disposable income, which fell to record lows in the 1990s as a result of the stock bubble, fell even lower during the housing bubble. Since 2004, that rate has fallen below 1 percent (see figure 4.3).

In this way, rising house prices led to more consumption,

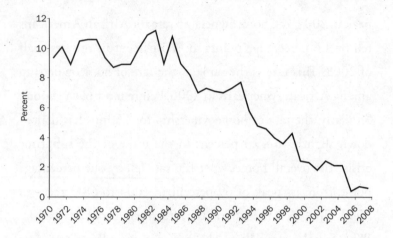

FIGURE 4.3 Saving as a Percentage of Disposable Income

Source: Bureau of Economic Analysis, National Income and Product Accounts.

which provided much of the fuel for economic growth during these years. Homeowners spent their newfound equity almost as quickly as it was created. By the end of 2006, average homeowners owned just 50.2 percent of their homes; their counterparts ten years earlier had owned 57.6 percent of their homes. Ten years before that, average homeowners had a 67.6 percent stake in their homes.[9] This plunge in equity occurred despite the fact that the overall population was aging, and much of the baby boom cohort was beginning to retire.

Housing-driven consumption—together with the jobs in

construction, real estate, and mortgage banking directly generated by the housing boom—lifted the economy out of the 2001 recession and the slump that followed. But the economy wasn't on a sustainable growth path. The housing bubble created the illusion of prosperity, and many people had a stake in perpetuating it. Like the alcoholic who copes with a hangover by guzzling another drink, Americans were using the housing bubble to recover from the effects of the stock bubble collapse. It was inevitable that this situation would end badly.

CHAPTER 5

The Final Collapse

As I learned back in the 1990s, it's difficult to predict the timing of a financial collapse. I first recognized the stock bubble in early 1997, and for the next three years, I was expecting a collapse within six months. Likewise with the housing bubble, although I knew better than to say anything publicly about when it would come. The bubble was evident as early as 2002, but it was impossible to determine how long house prices would continue to diverge from their long-term trend level. There were, after all, many moving parts. How long would investors continue to gamble recklessly? How long would Alan Greenspan, a longstanding inflation hawk, with his strongly negative view of inflation and its effects on society, keep interest rates so close to zero?

There were surprises in the markets, too, most notably a

drop in long-term interest rates and the continued strength of the dollar. In June 2003, long-term rates fell to 3 percent, the lowest rate since 1956, and remained at historically low levels for the rest of the bubble period. Even so, the dollar continued to remain hugely overvalued, primarily against East Asian currencies, during this period. This overvaluation pushed the trade deficit to new heights.

Normally, it would be difficult to explain the coincidence of a strong dollar and extraordinarily low interest rates. But the same factor was keeping both the dollar up and long-term interests down. Foreign central banks were buying massive quantities of dollars and using much of them to buy long-term Treasury bonds.

As an investment decision, it seemed foolhardy to hold dollar-based assets in these years. The huge trade deficit indicated that the dollar would subsequently fall in value (as it did against the euro from 2002 to 2006). Investors typically receive higher interest rates to compensate for this risk, but those higher rates didn't materialize. As we have seen, foreign central banks may have been more interested in continuing their exports to the United States than in profiting off their currency bets.

Cheap imports from Asia kept U.S. inflation low, and the surge in imports continued to displace domestic manufacturing, keeping the U.S. labor market weak. These outcomes made

Greenspan comfortable with keeping interest rates low. With no evidence of inflation, he felt little pressure to raise interest rates. These unexpected developments helped to maintain low interest rates far longer than almost anyone expected, providing further fuel for the housing bubble.

But the continued growth of the bubble wasn't a matter only of Federal Reserve policy. It also required other financial institutions to make or buy loans that would never be paid off. Even though large banks generally don't make a policy of throwing their money in the garbage, they were happy to do so in the peak years of the housing bubble.

THE EXCESSES
OF THE HOUSING BUBBLE

As house prices grew further out of line with the fundamentals, such as income and population growth, the financial industry created ever more innovative instruments, including nonstandard mortgages, to support continued growth.

Until the mid-1990s, the vast majority of home mortgages had fixed interest rates, but the number and share of adjustable-rate mortgages grew during the boom. Between 2004 and 2006, they made up almost 35 percent of all mortgages, after previously averaging less than 10 percent. This growth was even more striking because long-term interest rates were extraordinarily low during these years, meaning that home-buyers could get a fixed-rate mortgage at a very good price. ARMs didn't provide the security of fixed-rate mortgages, because the monthly payment fluctuated with market condi-tions. Moreover, many of the ARMs issued during this period started with below market "teaser rates" that would reset to higher levels after two years, even if interest rates didn't rise. Although teaser rates were especially common in the subprime segment of the mortgage market, where prospective buyers of-ten had poor credit histories, subprime mortgages were often issued to buyers with solid credit histories as well.[1] The interest rates on subprime loans were typically two to four percentage points higher than the interest rate on prime loans.

The subprime market exploded during this period, rising from less than 9 percent of the market in 2002 to 25 percent four years later. In addition to this explosion in subprime loans, there was a boom in the intermediate Alt-A mortgage category, which served homebuyers with mixed credit records or those who had provided incomplete documentation of income and assets. In many cases, the quality of these loans was even more questionable than that of subprime loans. Although it's dif-ficult to say for sure, many (perhaps most) of these loans were probably issued for the purchase of investment properties.

Many of these loans had the status of "liar loans," mean-ing that borrowers simply wrote down the numbers needed to qualify for a mortgage, regardless of reality and often at the suggestion of the mortgage broker. Many buyers used Alt-A loans to borrow the full value of the purchase price, or in some cases even a few percentage points more than the purchase price. Also, many of the Alt-A mortgages issued between 2005 and 2007 were interest-only loans, which required borrowers to pay only the interest on their mortgages.

Another mortgage innovation of this period, option ARMs, were even more lax. These loans allowed borrowers to make only nominal payments on their mortgages, letting unpaid interest be added to the principle, at least until a reset date. For both interest-only loans and option ARMs, the most common reset period was five years. Although these loans allowed borrowers to make lower payments for a period of time, the cost was significantly higher interest payments after the reset period. Because many of these borrowers would have difficulty making normal monthly payments, it should have been obvious that they would be greater default risks when the resets arrived.

Apparently, this notion came as a surprise to the top management at Wachovia Bank, the country's fifth largest bank. Losses on bad loans pushed Wachovia close to insolvency and led the bank to seek new management. Wachovia asked an independent consulting firm to determine which factors led to its problems. After talking with the bank's top financial officer and top risk officer, the consulting firm offered the following conclusion:

> Wachovia noted that some portion of the population which is attracted to the option ARM product seemed to "know something that underwriters didn't." So, based on FICO scores or loan-to-value these borrowers looked the same as other borrowers that opt for more traditional mortgages. However, Wachovia believes that the option ARM borrower seems to have more propensity to default, perhaps due to an impending job loss or other circumstance that they are aware of, but is not shown in a credit profile."[2]

In other words, borrowers eager to obtain low initial payments, whatever the long-term costs might be, were disproportionately people who faced immediate financial problems. Somehow Wachovia invested heavily in option ARM mortgages without realizing that these clients were high-risk borrowers.

Wachovia wasn't the only bank whose management didn't understand these risks. Fannie Mae, the mortgage giant that created the secondary mortgage market, was also heavily invested in subprime and Alt-A debt in the late stages of the housing bubble. It bought several hundred billion dollars in mortgage-backed securities in both categories. According to its president, Fannie Mae felt comfortable acquiring this debt, even as late as 2007. After conducting stress tests of its holdings of mortgage-backed securities, Fannie concluded that it would still break even if house prices fell by 5 percent annually for two consecutive years.[3]

Stress tests are supposed to assess how a financial institution's assets will perform under the worst plausible scenarios. Apparently, the worst plausible scenario that Fannie Mae's top management could envision at the peak of the bubble was a 10-percent decline in house prices over two years. In fact, house prices nationwide fell close to 20 percent in the two years following their peak in 2006, and they will almost certainly fall further in the coming year. In the markets with heavy concentrations of subprime mortgages (such as San Diego, Los Angeles, and Las Vegas), prices had already dropped by more than 30 percent by the summer of 2008.

Meanwhile, nonstandard mortgages were proliferating. The subprime and Alt-A categories together comprised more than 40 percent of the loans issued at the peak of the bubble in 2006. Loans requiring limited documentation had expanded from 27 percent of the mortgages issued in 2001 to 44 percent in 2006. The share of homes purchased with 100 percent financing went from 3 percent in 2003 to 33 percent in 2006.[4]

This proliferation of high-risk loans should have been sufficient to signal regulators and investors that there was a serious problem. No one could seriously believe that the number of creditworthy people in the subprime category had more than doubled between 2002 and 2006, a period during which the

labor market remained weak and wages lagged behind inflation. The increase in subprime lending over these years was
itself an unmistakable warning sign of the problems in the
housing market. Instead of taking this warning, political leaders and industry cheerleaders celebrated the record rates of
homeownership.

WRONG INCENTIVES EVERYWHERE

The surge in high-risk loans was enabled by misplaced incentives throughout the industry, beginning with the appraisal
process. Appraisers typically operate as independent contractors and are hired by banks or mortgage issuers. In prior years,
banks would have valued an honest appraisal, because they
wanted to ensure that the collateral in the house would cover
the value of the loan if the homebuyer defaulted. However, during the years of the housing bubble, mortgage issuers earned
their money by issuing mortgages, not holding them, as the
overwhelming majority of new mortgages were quickly sold
in the **secondary market**. This meant that the issuers wanted
to make sure that appraisals would come in high enough to
justify the size of the mortgage. Instead of accurate appraisals,
they wanted the highest ones possible.

This bias was quickly passed through to the appraisers themselves. They realized that the bank wouldn't hire them again if

their appraisals were too low to allow mortgages to be issued. This meant that appraisers had a strong incentive to adopt a high-side bias. In this way, the appraisers played the same role in the housing bubble that auditors played in the stock bubble. Instead of presenting independent, disinterested assessments, they offered appraisals that served the interests of the parties that hired them. Once again, the simple way to avoid such **perverse incentives** is to require that an independent board pick the appraisers. In fact, this method is common with nonresidential real estate appraisals.

An even more important set of misplaced incentives existed in the secondary markets, whose very existence gave mortgage issuers incentives to approve bad loans. Because these issuers generally faced little risk once the mortgage was sold, their incentive was to issue as many mortgages as possible. They only had to ensure that these mortgages, on paper, were good enough to sell in the secondary market. Because the issuers know very well the criteria for resale, they made sure that their loans met those standards.

The next step was in the hands of the banks that bought and bundled the loans into mortgage-banked securities. These banks also made their money on the fees associated with this securitization process, not on holding the mortgage-backed securities themselves. This meant that the securitizers also had an incentive to maximize volume with little regard for the actual quality of the loans they were bundling or the underlying quality of the mortgage-backed securities they were issuing.

The banks' ability to sell mortgage-backed securities depended on their credit rating for their bonds. Here also perverse incentives played an important role. The bond rating agencies are paid by the banks requesting the rating. To avoid losing customers to their competitors, credit-rating agencies had a strong incentive to issue high ratings to the banks' securities. In at least some cases, higher-ups at the bond rating agencies overrode objections of lower-level analysts and insisted that mortgage-backed securities of questionable quality be given investment grades.[5]

This process was facilitated by the proliferation of new and more complex financial instruments and questionable accounting practices, innovations that took place in the middle of a housing bubble, when house prices were rising at near record rates. Both buyers and sellers were extrapolating from this period, effectively assuming that the bubble would persist and grow indefinitely.[6] The relevant regulatory agencies mostly looked the other way. Essentially, major banks were making multi-billion dollar transactions selling assets that neither they nor their customers understood.

There were other noteworthy twists to the speculative finance that helped create the current crisis. This period saw an enormous proliferation of **credit default swaps**, which were issued by major banks and other financial institutions as insurance against defaults on bonds. Credit default swaps allowed many smaller firms, as well as state and local governments, to sell their bonds more easily. Their credit was backed by the banks issuing the credit default swaps on their bonds. Credit default swaps were also issued against mortgage-backed securities and various derivative instruments, which facilitated the sale of mortgage-backed securities of questionable quality.

Credit default swaps came into existence in the late 1990s, but their use exploded during the peak years of the housing bubble. Their growth was facilitated by the fact that they were completely unregulated, the result of the zeal for deregulation in the 1990s.

In addition to providing a way to insure against bond defaults, credit default swaps also turned out to be a useful tool for speculation. Investors could bet on the probability that a particular bond would default. The Bank of International Settlements estimated the total notional value—that is, the amount of debt insured—of credit default swaps at more than $45 trillion in June of 2007.[7] Furthermore, because their issuance was largely unregulated, banks leveraged themselves very heavily in issuing credit default swaps that had notional values that could be several hundred times their capital.

Though not directly related to the mortgage market, another credit market innovation of this period was the **auction rate**

security. This financing tool replaced long-term bonds with a series of short-term financing issues. Instead of issuing 20- or 30-year bonds, a state or local government would use auction rate securities to refinance a loan at short intervals, typically 30 to 90 days. If the short-term interest rate stayed below the long-term interest rate at the time of the initial borrowing, this financing tool could allow for large gains. However, when short-term rates at these auctions rose, the issuers were exposed to substantial risks.

The major investment banks underwrote tens of billions of dollars worth of auction rate securities by state and local governments and other organizations during the years of the housing boom. Many of the issuers were relatively small cities with officials who almost certainly didn't understand the risks involved with these securities. When interest rates rose sharply in these auction markets in 2007, they posed a severe financial hardship for these cities.[8]

Underlying all these developments was an incentive structure that placed an enormous premium on short-term profits, often at the expense of longer-term profits or even longer-term corporate survival. Executives in the financial sector are paid in large part in bonuses based on how effectively they reach profit targets or stock options, the value of which are hugely responsive to short-term profits. In both cases, there's an enormous incentive to show short-term profits.

This arrangement gave managers little incentive to plan for the long-term health of their companies and encouraged all forms of risky behavior. The highest incomes flowed from generating large fees, even if there would be losses from the assets being sold. This was certainly the case with the issuance of highly questionable subprime and Alt-A mortgages, as well as credit default swaps. In these cases, the underlying assets were often very risky and could lead to large losses, but the fees from issuing and bundling mortgages and from selling credit default swaps led to large short-term profits.

Largely because of these incentive structures, many of the leading figures at the worst financial institutions became enormously wealthy, even as they wrecked their companies. For example, Angelo Mozila, the CEO of Countrywide Financial, the nation's largest originator of subprime mortgages, earned several hundred million dollars in compensation over the last decade. After the crash, his company was taken over by Bank of America at a bargain-basement price.

Similarly, James E. Cayne, the boss who led Bear Stearns to bankruptcy, pocketed hundreds of millions of dollars for his work. The same is undoubtedly true for many hedge-fund managers who received 20 percent of large gains during the good years, but who are now watching their clients lose much of their investment as the market turns down.

The top executives at Citigroup all earned tens of millions

in annual compensation as the bank pushed the financial envelope with complex financial instruments and auction rate securities. When these deals went bad, Citigroup stock lost 80 percent of its value. The loss might have been even greater if former Treasury Secretary Robert Rubin hadn't used his connections to arrange for an injection of capital from the Middle East and elsewhere.

When coupled with a weak regulatory system, this compensation structure gives executives enormous incentive to use financial engineering to gain quick profits, regardless of long-term costs. In 1996, the financial sector accounted for less than 16 percent of corporate profits. By 2004, the sector accounted for more than 25 percent of corporate profits. As we now know, much of what financial corporations booked as profits in these years was illusory. Their "profits" were fees on transactions that would eventually lead to large losses for their companies. But these profits provided the basis for large rewards for the big movers and shakers in the financial industry.

THE MELTDOWN

The bubble began to unravel after house prices peaked in the middle of 2006. This led to a rapid rise in default rates, especially in the subprime market. Although the worst abuses in the mortgage market were, indeed, in the subprime segment, the main reason defaults were initially concentrated so heavily there was because these homeowners were the most vulnerable. When they couldn't make their mortgage payments, they didn't have retirement accounts to draw on or family members to borrow from. Falling house prices destroyed whatever equity they had in their homes, at which point many subprime homeowners had little choice but to default on their mortgages.

The decline in house prices rather than the resets to higher interest rates is really the central issue in the story of the subprime crisis. Close to 10 percent of the subprime ARMs issued in 2006 went into default within a year of issuance, long before any of them reset to higher rates. Homebuyers found themselves over their heads almost from the beginning. The only way they could afford their home was if house prices continued to rise. When prices turned downward in the middle of 2006, millions of recent homebuyers suddenly faced serious difficulties holding onto their homes. The problem was made worse by ARMs resetting to higher rates. But if house prices had continued to rise at double-digit rates, these resets wouldn't have led to a tidal wave of foreclosures. Instead of letting the banks foreclose on their houses, homeowners with equity in their homes could have borrowed against the equity or sold their houses for a profit.

Many of the subprime loans that began going bad in 2006 and 2007 were mortgages used to refinance homes. Subprime lenders aggressively, and often deceptively, offered to refinance loans so that low-income homeowners could pay their bills or make big purchases. As a result of these new subprime loans, families who had been relatively secure financially suddenly faced the loss of their homes.

The spread of defaults in the subprime market led to a sharp reduction in the valuation of mortgage-backed securities. These securities, of course, contained substantial quantities of subprime mortgages and derivative instruments. That sharp reduction led to the series of credit squeezes that hit financial markets beginning in the winter of 2007. Investors had little confidence in the quality of a wide range of assets and institutions, especially because they couldn't determine the extent to which these assets and institutions were exposed to bad mortgage debt.

Although the housing data began to turn downward in the summer of 2006, financial problems began to make headlines only in February 2007, when there were sharp declines in stock markets across the world. China led the way with an 8 percent one-day price decline, but markets across Europe and the United States saw single-day drops of 3 percent or more.

In the wake of this market turmoil, Federal Reserve Board Chairman Ben Bernanke reassured the public about the state of the economy. In testimony the following month, he told Congress:

At this juncture, however, the impact on the broader economy and financial markets of the problems in the subprime market seems likely to be contained. In particular, mortgages to prime borrowers and fixed-rate mortgages to all classes of borrowers continue to perform well, with low rates of delinquency.[9]

Reassured by the Fed chair, as well as by the soothing words from Treasury Secretary Henry Paulson and other prominent economists, the financial markets settled down. The U.S. stock market quickly recovered its lost ground, reaching record highs by July.

This was the lull before the storm. In late July, the stock market again plunged. The markets recognized that major banks were facing serious write-downs due to their holdings of bad mortgages, mortgage-backed securities, and more complex derivative instruments. It became clear that the financial problems were not confined to the subprime mortgage market and that these problems would have a substantial impact on both the financial system and the economy as a whole.

What those impacts would be remained uncertain, however, and this uncertainty began to take its toll. One measure of uncertainty in financial markets is the spread, or gap, between the rate that banks charge each other for short-term loans, called LIBOR, and the rate on U.S. Treasury bills of the same duration. Ordinarily this gap is relatively small, typically in the range of 0.1 to 0.2 percentage points, because there's little risk associated with lending to major banks. However, it jumped in August of 2007 to more than 1 percentage point, reflecting the fact that banks no longer trusted each other to repay short-term loans. Because the banks that borrow in the LIBOR market are among the largest in the world, this situation was truly extraordinary.

In August 2007, the Fed implicitly acknowledged that the economy faced serious problems as a result of the housing meltdown. It had raised interest rates at each of its meetings since June 2004, but the rate hikes were put on hold in March 2007, following the first wave of turmoil in February. In August, the Fed reversed course and implemented a rate cut between regular meetings, a very rare move.

More important, the Fed established a special "term auction facility" because it could no longer be assumed that major banks could repay loans. That facility auctioned off loan funds from the Fed for periods of up to 90 days. For banks, these loans were an alternative to borrowing from the Fed's discount window. Banks that are short of their required reserves regularly take advantage of the Fed's discount window to borrow reserves for short periods of time. A major advantage of the term auction facility, relative to the discount window, is that money could be borrowed secretly, because the Fed didn't identify the banks that received the loans. By contrast, the

Fed reports all borrowing that occurs through the discount window.

The Fed justified this secret lending by saying that financial markets attach a stigma to borrowing at the discount window and that fear of incurring this stigma would discourage banks from borrowing reserves and increasing the liquidity of the system. The secrecy of the term auction facility would instead allow banks to borrow without facing any penalty from financial markets.

Few commentators pointed out the major irony of this policy. The mostly conservative economists who run the Fed strongly advocate the wisdom of the market, yet they created a mechanism that secretly circumvented the market's judgment. If the Fed believed that the market responds rationally, there should be no reason for the secrecy. The Fed's action showed that they didn't trust the market's wisdom.[10]

THE HOUSING MARKET
AND THE ECONOMY

By 2007, the housing market was in full meltdown, and housing promoters were suddenly coming to grips with the fact that prices could fall. Angelo Mozilo, the CEO of the mortgage giant Countrywide Financial, said in a July conference call that house prices were falling "almost like never before, with the exception of the Great Depression."[11] Comparisons to the Great Depression soon became common, but now they were coming out of the mouths of former bubble-deniers.

By every measure, the housing sector had taken a sharp downturn. By the second quarter of 2007, construction spending on new single-family homes was already down by more than 30 percent from its peak in the fourth quarter of 2005. Sales of new and existing homes also showed sharp downturns, and the foreclosure rate began to soar.

The falloff in the housing sector became a major drag on overall economic growth, and by December 2007, the private sector was shedding jobs. One by one, leading economic experts switched their tune from "the economy is strong" to "the economy needs stimulus." This parade eventually included most of the country's leading economic forecasters, including Fed Chair Ben Bernanke, Treasury Secretary Henry Paulson, and even President Bush himself. In true Washington fashion, mistakes were never acknowledged. Earlier misinformation and even outright deceptions were simply ignored.

The *Washington Post* deserves special mention in this "admit no errors" world. On January 11, 2008, its lead editorial warned against the rush to enact a fiscal stimulus:

> There is not yet any proof of a recession, defined as two straight quarters of negative growth; Mr. Bernanke said yesterday that the

economy probably grew "at a moderate pace" in the past three months. Nor is there any consensus that a recession, if one comes, will be severe; Goldman Sachs thinks it's likely to be short and mild.[12]

Just eight days later, the headline of the lead editorial was "Calculating the Stimulus: Everyone Agrees the Economy Needs a Boost . . ."[13]

There was renewed turmoil in world financial markets, with the spread between the LIBOR rate and the federal funds rate again increasing to extraordinary levels. Bernanke implemented another emergency rate cut, this time lowering the federal funds rate by three quarters of a percentage point. It was becoming increasingly difficult to smile and maintain the assertion that everything was fine.

The next big step along these lines came in March 2008. Bear Stearns, one of the country's largest investment banks, suddenly found itself facing collapse. There had been rumors about the impact of its losses in subprime mortgage-backed securities, which finally led to the collapse of a multi-billion dollar fund that it managed. Fears over the extent of the eventual losses impeded its efforts to borrow.

The Fed again jumped in to save the day. It gave a short-term loan to Bear Stearns and arranged a buyout by J.P. Morgan Chase, one of the few major banks that wasn't already hurting. The buyout was noteworthy because it came with a guarantee from the Fed of $30 billion against Bear Stearns's assets. J.P.

Morgan originally agreed to pay $2 a share for stock that had sold for $170 a share a year earlier, implying a purchase price for Bear Stearns of $270 million. After some Bear Stearns stockholders threatened legal action, the price was raised to $10 a share, or $1.35 billion.

The Fed effectively made J.P. Morgan pay for the higher share price by stipulating that it would incur the first $1 billion in losses on Bear's assets, with the value of the guarantee reduced to $29 billion. Even with this stipulation, the Fed was still being very generous with Bear Stearns's shareholders. J.P. Morgan could have negotiated to buy Bear Stearns without the Fed's intervention. The only reason it was willing to buy at all was that the deal came with a huge guarantee from the Fed. In effect, Bear Stearns's shareholders received $1.35 billion, not for the value of their stock, but rather for the value of that Fed guarantee.

This wasn't the only goody Bernanke offered the major investment banks. He also allowed them the enormously valuable privilege of borrowing from the Fed at below-market rates, much as commercial banks do. In exchange for this privilege, however, commercial banks must keep a fraction of their deposits on reserve with the Fed, where they collect no interest. Commercial banks are also subject to extensive regulatory scrutiny from the Fed. Now Bernanke was giving investment banks the same privilege without those conditions. He went further by establishing the "Term Securities Lending Facility," which allowed the investment banks to borrow from the Fed using the same sort of secret auction process that he had created for the commercial banks the previous year.

THE MELTDOWN GETS SERIOUS

The measures taken in March 2008 had little lasting effect. The tidal wave of defaults led to even larger losses at banks and other financial institutions. By July, bad debt had pushed both Fannie Mae and Freddie Mac to the edge of insolvency. Congress renewed its commitment to these mortgage giants by passing a housing bill, and the Fed opened its discount window, but these steps proved insufficient. On September 7, 2008, both institutions were put into conservatorship, effectively a form of bankruptcy that placed them under the control of the federal government. The government committed up to $200 billion to cover the debts of the two institutions.

Even though the collapse of Fannie and Freddie was an extraordinary event, it was only the beginning of that month's drama. The next week, Lehman Brothers, the weakest of the four remaining major investment banks, went bankrupt. Betting that the financial system could withstand the shock from Lehman's collapse, Paulson and Bernanke declined to bail out the company.

This proved to be a bad bet. Lehman was much more integral to the financial system than had been apparent. It was the primary broker for major hedge funds, many of which quickly sold shares to maintain liquidity. Financial markets in the United States and around the world plunged, and the gap between the LIBOR and the Treasury bill rate jumped to 2 percentage points.

The next day, September 16, 2008, the Fed and the Treasury had to decide what to do about AIG, the country's largest insurer. Like Bear Stearns, AIG had issued trillions of dollars worth of credit default swaps, but it had no capacity to support the swaps in the event of a systematic collapse. Paulson and Bernanke decided to save AIG. The Treasury lent it $85 billion and took almost an 80 percent stake in the company.

At this point, Paulson and Bernanke changed course. After having consistently minimized the extent of the problem, they both told congressional leaders that the economy was on the edge of collapse. News accounts reported that House Speaker Nancy Pelosi and the rest of the leadership looked shaken after the meeting.

On September 20, Secretary Paulson revealed his plan to save the banking system. It was a three-page document that essentially called on Congress to turn over $700 billion, which he would use to buy bad debts from banks. The plan explicitly stated that his purchases were not to be subject to any review or legal action.

This bailout proposal prompted outrage across the country. The public couldn't understand why they should be asked to bail out some of the very richest people in the country, people who were in trouble as a result of their own greed and incompetence. Calls and emails to members of Congress were running more than 99 percent against the proposal, according to many members.

By contrast, virtually the entire political establishment from both parties and the news media lined up behind the bill's immediate passage. President Bush went on national television and warned that another Great Depression was possible if the bill was voted down. The move was unprecedented; usually a president's opponents claim that his policies, if approved, will bring on a depression. Now Bush was warning that only urgent action would spare us from the effects of his own misrule.

Rarely has there been such a sharp divide between elite and public opinion on such an important measure. When the House initially voted down the bailout on September 29, the elites were furious. *New York Times* columnist Thomas Friedman demanded that Congress "rescue the rescue," complaining that the House had rejected "a complex rescue package because some voters, whom I fear also don't understand, swamped them with phone calls."[14]

Most other newspapers were also filled with editorials, columns, and new stories making the same argument. The stock market plummeted immediately after the House vote. This plunge was yet another argument mustered by the elite, who claimed that the bailout opponents were responsible for the loss of more than $1 trillion in stock wealth.

Despite the purported urgency of the situation, Paulson refused to give ground to the objections being raised to the bailout bill. For example, he rejected a proposal to allow bankruptcy judges to rewrite the terms on mortgage debt, just as they do on other debts. This measure could have allowed hundreds of thousands of American families facing foreclosure to stay in their homes. Paulson also refused to allow serious restrictions on executive compensation. These restrictions would have prevented executives from being rewarded for their incompetence and would have assured taxpayers that their dollars were not making the rich even richer. In reality, the impact of the bill's language on executive compensation would be virtually zero, as was noted in several press accounts published after the bill was passed.[15]

Remarkably, the stock markets fell even more sharply after the bill's final passage than it had after the House initially voted the bill down. This time, however, no one in the media blamed Congress for the decline. The problems were global; financial markets and banks everywhere were hurting. Even more remarkable was the fact that Paulson took no immediate action on his bailout plan. Having warned that every day's delay in taking action could lead to serious damage, Paulson did nothing in the week after Congress gave him the authority he requested.

When he did act, Paulson chose a completely different plan than the one he had insisted was so urgent. Instead of buying up the bad assets held by banks, Paulson announced that he would directly inject capital into the banking system and take an equity stake in exchange. This was truly an extraordinary turn of events. Perhaps the most conservative administration in a century was partially nationalizing the nation's banks.

THE MELTDOWN
AND THE ECONOMY

By October 2008, the time of this writing, there was little doubt that the economy was in a recession and that it would likely be a serious one. Even in the best-case scenario, in which the immediate financial problems are contained, the economy would have to cope with the loss of $8 trillion in housing bubble wealth.

Consumption has held up remarkably well, but it's virtually inevitable that households will begin to cut back after widespread and massive loss of wealth from the housing crash.

In fact, the reputable Case-Shiller index indicates that families have already lost close to $5 trillion ($70,000 per homeowner) as a result of this crash. If the housing market corrects to its trend level, the loss will be $8 trillion, or $110,000 per homeowner.

This loss of wealth will leave tens of millions of homeowners with little or no equity in their homes. Such homeowners will no longer be able to borrow against their equity to support their previous levels of consumption. Furthermore, families who thought they had accumulated substantial equity in their homes to support their retirement will find that they have very little actual wealth. An analysis of late baby boomers (ages 45–54), found that the median household in this age group will have less than $100,000 in wealth, including equity in their home, assuming that house prices stabilize in 2009.[16]

In short, the housing crash is likely to lead to a serious economic downturn. Consumption will decline, the financial sector will be badly crippled for years to come, and millions of families will see their plans for a secure retirement destroyed. The economy faces a serious and immediate crisis, but it's not too early to start thinking about ways to rebuild it on a sounder footing.

CHAPTER 6

Beyond the Bubble Economy

In the wake of the housing bubble collapse, the United States needs sensible policies, not only to alleviate the financial pain the crisis has created, but also to build an economy that goes beyond these boom-and-bust cycles.

The first and perhaps most important reform that we need to our financial system is a clear and serious commitment by the Fed to combat asset bubbles. Having just gone through the rise and demise of massive ones in the stock and housing markets, investors may have learned something about the importance of relating prices to fundamentals, at least in these two markets, if not more broadly. However, people who control large amounts of money have shown themselves to be incredibly foolish. For this reason, unless the Fed takes action to prevent financial bubbles, it is likely that we will see more of them.

The Fed has a wide variety of tools it could use to rein in bubbles. The first tool is very simple: talk. The Federal Reserve chair regularly testifies before Congress and frequently speaks in other public forums. The point here is not to mumble the words "irrational exuberance" as if they were the expression of a private opinion. The point is to lay out evidence that cannot be ignored. If the Fed chair used his public forums to explicitly lay out the case for a financial bubble and the potential risks it poses, that act would have an impact on the relevant market.

For example, in 1998 and 1999, Alan Greenspan could have explained that price-to-earning ratios in the stock market were inconsistent with any plausible projection of corporate profit growth. He could have pointed out that unless stockholders were prepared to hold stock for very low returns, prices were far above levels consistent with shareholder expectations of returns. If Greenspan had made these arguments with the supporting charts and data, the markets would likely have responded with substantial sell-offs.

Similarly, if Greenspan had pointed out in 2002–2006 that real house prices had risen more than 70 percent after staying flat for 100 years, many Americans would have paid attention. He also could have pointed out that many of the hold-ers of mortgage-backed securities and derivative instruments were taking serious risks. And he could have said that the Fed would aid neither the banks that engaged in reckless practices nor their creditors.

Statements of this sort might not directly affect the willingness of families to buy homes, but they almost certainly would have affected the willingness of banks and other financial institutions to lend those families money. The top managers of banks and investment funds would face some serious questions, and possibly even lawsuits threatening personal liability, if they lost their institutions tens of billions of dollars after ignoring explicit warnings from the Fed chairman. Economists and financial analysts can certainly differ on the state of the economy, but simply ignoring clear warnings from the Fed would be incredibly irresponsible.

The Fed can also use its substantial regulatory authority to rein in bubbles. In the case of the stock market, the main tool is the **margin requirement** for borrowing to buy stock. By itself, raising the margin requirement would have relatively little impact, because only a small portion of stock is purchased with margin loans. But doing so would call attention to the Fed's view that the stock market is overvalued.

The Fed's regulatory powers in the housing markets are more extensive. During the housing bubble, it could have put forward regulations (as it has recently done) to prevent the issuance of some of the worst subprime loans. Banks under the Fed's control account for only about 30 percent of new mortgages, but the standards set by the Fed likely would have been adopted by other regulatory institutions and probably would have become the norm for loans to enter mortgage pools in the secondary market. These standards would have limited some of the worst practices that both ensnared homeowners and helped fuel the housing bubble.

Of course, the Fed can always raise interest rates to rein in financial bubbles. But this extremely blunt instrument also has the effect of slowing the economy and throwing people out of work. For this reason, the Fed should be reluctant to use higher interest rates as a weapon against asset bubbles. The damage from a housing bubble is so extensive, however, that if the Fed's other tools fail to stem its growth, the Fed should raise interest rates.

Compared to the housing and stock-market bubbles of the last decade, bubbles in other areas of the economy don't pose the same threat of instability. For example, if the price of platinum were to triple over a fairly short period of time, most sectors of the economy would be unaffected. Furthermore, because only a small segment of the population has either a direct or an indirect stake in platinum, a run-up in its price is unlikely to have any noticeable effect on aggregate consumption. In the case of the platinum market, the Fed's "bubbles come, bubbles go" philosophy might be appropriate. But this philosophy clearly is inappropriate for the stock and housing markets. The Fed must count the prevention of bubbles in these markets, and possibly other key sectors of the economy, among its responsibilities.

On at least two occasions, the 1987 stock market crash and the collapse of Long-Term Capital, Greenspan claimed that his responsibilities required him to intervene to prevent asset prices from falling as a result of (presumably) irrational market forces. But no economic theory shows that the economy suffers more harm from asset prices pushed too low by irrational market sentiments than from asset prices pushed too high by those same sentiments.

Lawrence Meyer, a former Federal Reserve Board governor, once argued that the Fed lacked the political independence to explicitly attack an asset bubble, even if it determined that it was the appropriate course of action for the economy. Noting that attacking the stock bubble would have destroyed trillions of dollars of wealth, Meyer commented that this was "a politically untenable situation for a central bank to be in."[1] If the central bank lacks the necessary political independence from Wall Street to effectively manage the economy, it must be reorganized to do so.

PRICING THE DOLLAR RIGHT

One of the biggest forces distorting the U.S. economy over the last decade has been the overvalued dollar. The high dollar was a conscious policy of the Clinton administration in the years after Robert Rubin became Treasury secretary. A strong dollar sounds appealing as a political ploy, and it has some beneficial short-term effects. Specifically, it makes imports cheaper for people in the United States, which raises our standard of living and reduces inflation.

However, these benefits are short term in the very same way that some tax cuts are. Both can lead to unsustainable deficits. In the case of tax cuts, interest costs on the debt become unbearable, forcing tax increases or spending cuts. In the case of the overvalued dollar, a trade deficit results. U.S. consumers will buy more imports rather than higher-priced domestically produced goods, while foreign consumers will buy fewer U.S. exports.

Like large budget deficits, large trade deficits are unsustainable. Eventually, the dollar must fall to bring the trade deficit down.

Furthermore, as discussed in chapter 3, a large trade deficit means that national savings must be negative. That is, the government must run a very large budget deficit, household savings must be extremely low (possibly negative), or some combination of the two, as is presently the case. Clearly, large budget deficits or very low household saving rates for long periods are undesirable. If the country has a large trade deficit, however, there is no alternative.

Fluctuations in the value of the dollar affect some workers more than others. Workers in the manufacturing sector, for example, compete directly in the global economy. Other workers, particularly highly paid professionals, such as doctors, lawyers, economists, and accountants, enjoy substantial protection from international competition. As we have seen, an overvalued dollar effectively puts downward pressure on the wages of the workers who are most directly subject to international competition—usually those who tend to have no college degree. But workers who are largely protected from international competition—those who tend to be highly educated—benefit from a strong dollar by being able to buy imports at comparatively low prices. For this reason, a strong dollar effectively redistributes income from less educated workers to the most highly educated workers. This redistribution, in turn, makes broad prosperity—which once characterized our economy and produced a host of social and economic benefits—much more difficult to achieve.

Given that an overvalued dollar is unsustainable and has substantial consequences for the distribution of wealth, the Fed and the Treasury should recognize their responsibility to ensure that the value of the dollar be sustained at a reasonable level.

FIXING THE FINANCIAL SECTOR

The financial sector is in desperate need of a makeover. Finance serves a central role in the economy, steering money from savers to borrowers. But finance is an intermediate good, not an end in itself. We might want more or better houses, health care, and food, but we have no reason to want more financial transactions. The fewer people and resources we need to do our banking, to provide insurance, and to meet our other financial needs, the better off we are. We want to structure the financial system to maximize its efficiency, not to drain the economy.

The first lesson to learn from the bubble economy is that we must set up the financial sector to give the proper incentives. The opposite was true in the case of the stock bubble, when auditors had a perverse incentive to bend the rules because the companies they were auditing hired and paid them.

Subsequent reforms helped limit creative accounting by making top corporate officers more directly responsible for their financial statements. However, the limited independence of auditors means that they still do not provide as effective a check on improper accounting as they could. The solution is to require a third party—such as a stock exchange or a governmental body—to assign auditors to companies. The companies would continue to pay for audits, on the basis of a standard rate structure, but they would not get to select their auditor. This system would eliminate the conflicts of interest that allowed for Enron-type fraud and that persist today.

Under the proposed system, firms could fire auditors they consider incompetent or ill performing, but the independent body would pick the replacement auditor. The rules should be structured so that occasional removal of an auditor would not be difficult. But they should make it impossible for companies to continually replace auditors—that is, shop for an auditor who will accept improper accounting.

Like the lack of strict audits during the stock bubble, the lack of credible appraisals during the housing bubble can be attributed to a perverse incentive. Because banks wanted to issue loans, they had no incentive to hire appraisers who made low appraisals. The appraisers, who usually work as independent contractors, recognized this fact and made a practice of supplying high appraisals.

Again, the solution is the formation of an independent body. A local board, public or private, would keep a list of approved appraisers. Banks would call the board to request appraisals, for which they would be charged a standard fee. Banks could request multiple appraisals, but they could play no role in selecting the appraisers.

The problem of perverse incentives also arises with bond-rating agencies, which banks and corporations pay to rate their bonds. The way things have been, if the bond-rating agency issues an unfavorable rating, it risks losing the client's business. Here, again, a requirement that the rater be selected independently could reduce or eliminate the conflict of interest inherent in the relationship. If a corporation knows that it cannot expect more sympathetic treatment by requesting a new rating, it's far less likely to do so.

On their own, markets may be able to address other issues that fed the stock and housing bubbles. Consider the secondary market that gave mortgage issuers little incentive to ensure that the loans they made could be paid off. Issuers could dump bad mortgages in the secondary market only because a vast pool of buyers for mortgage-backed securities accepted the assessments of the bond-rating agencies that stated they were getting high-quality debt. If the bond-rating agencies had seriously scrutinized these securities, they would have issued lower ratings in many cases. With the lower ratings, the mortgage-backed securities would have been much harder to sell. If the securitizers couldn't count on selling their mortgage-backed securities, they would be much more careful in reviewing the loans that they purchased initially. Consequently, issuers would be forced to pay more attention to the quality of the loans they make.

In short, if the rules are structured to ensure that bond-rating agencies make a serious effort to evaluate the quality of loans, the market should act to prevent a proliferation of poor-quality loans. An additional element of insurance in this process might be desirable. If issuers were required to maintain a partial interest in loans sold in the secondary market, they would have a further incentive to take the quality of loans seriously.

Other important regulatory issues have arisen in the context of the recent asset bubbles. There's no question that the growth of investment banks, hedge funds, and other largely unregulated pools of capital poses serious problems for the stability of the financial system. When Greenspan intervened in the unraveling of the Long-Term Capital hedge fund in 1998, and the Fed rushed to the rescue of the investment banks and their creditors in 2008, the threats to the financial system may have been large enough to warrant these interventions. But the fact that such interventions became necessary is a testament to the failure of regulation in the first place. The government can't prevent financial companies and wealthy investors from engaging in risky speculation, nor should it try. But it should clearly signal that it won't support such speculation as it effectively did with those high-profile interventions.

The clearest signal of intent would be better oversight of commercial banks and much more serious oversight of investment banks. Because the large investment banks have become central to the financial system—too big to fail—their dealings must be subject to the same sort of oversight as the commercial banks. This scrutiny would include daily oversight of their transactions, restrictions on leverage, and reserve requirements to effectively cover the cost of the implicit guarantees provided by the Fed. (With the recent restructuring of investment banks as subsidiaries of bank-holding companies, the investment bank components of these companies must be carefully regulated.)

Investment banks will undoubtedly resist more regulation, but it can be made completely voluntary. Essentially, the Fed can offer the new regulatory structure as a quid pro quo. If the investment banks agree to the structure, they will have access to the discount window. Moreover, their creditors will enjoy the implicit protection that the creditors of Bear Stearns enjoyed when that bank effectively became insolvent.

If, on the contrary, the investment banks don't agree to the new regulatory structure, they will receive no money from the Fed, either directly through the discount window or indirectly through banks that are part of the Federal Reserve System. Furthermore, if they become insolvent, the Fed will guarantee that it will do absolutely nothing to protect them or their creditors.

As a further check on speculation, the government can tax

gambling in financial assets in the same way that it taxes gambling at casinos or on racehorses. Given the enormous volume of trading in financial assets, even a very modest tax would raise enormous sums of money. A tax of 0.25 percent on each purchase or sale of a share of stock, along with scaled tax rates on other financial assets—for example, the tax on the purchase or sale of an option of credit default swap might be 0.01 percent of the price—can easily raise $150 billion a year, or 1 percent of GDP.[2]

A tax rate of this magnitude would raise transaction costs to the levels of the mid-1980s or early 1990s. But it would have almost no impact on typical savers or firms using financial markets to raise capital. For a person holding stock for five to ten years, the proposed tax would be almost invisible. If you bought $10,000 worth of stock while employed, the tax would cost you $25. If you sold the stock 10 years later for $20,000, you would pay $50 in tax. In both cases, the tax is likely to be less than the commission charged by the brokerage that handles the transaction. It is certainly less than the commission you would have paid on the transaction in 1980 or even 1990.

Even a modest tax, however, would be a serious cost for people buying and selling stock by the day or hour. For these people, the proposed tax is likely to absorb much of their expected profit. The government would collect considerable money from these frequent traders, just as it does from people who gamble at casinos or play state lotteries. The tax would also lead to a substantial reduction in the volume of trading—a positive development from the standpoint of the economy and society as a whole.

We have a seriously bloated financial sector that is absorbing an increasing share of the economy's resources. If a modest financial tax reduces the size of this sector, the workers who are no longer busy designing complex financial instruments might instead be engaged in more productive tasks, such as designing new software or fuel-efficient cars. Moreover, the revenues generated from a financial transactions tax can be used for many useful proposes, such as health care, education, public infrastructure, or even a progressive tax cut.

HOLDING THE INCOMPETENTS ACCOUNTABLE

Economists usually argue that employers must be able to fire poor-performing workers. But economists seem to think that firing is only needed as a disciplinary tool for custodians, factory workers, and schoolteachers. When it comes to more highly paid jobs (including their own), economists seem extremely tolerant of incompetence. In the case of the housing and stock bubbles, such incompetence was spewing from all corners. These bubbles couldn't have grown as much as they did, nor caused as much damage, if many professional analysts of the economy and the stock and housing markets had been doing their jobs correctly.

Recognizing both the stock and housing bubbles was easy. In the case of the stock bubble, price-to-earnings ratios had risen to levels that were inconsistent with plausible projections of future profit growth. Analysts had to believe that investors were willing to accept extremely low rates of return on stock—an implausible view given the irrational exuberance of the time—or that the market was in a bubble and prices would tumble.

In the case of housing, bubble-deniers had to believe that some unknown force had caused house prices to suddenly diverge from a 100-year trend. They also had to believe that a rapid and unprecedented rise in vacancy rates wouldn't affect prices. Finally, they had to believe that house sale prices were no longer connected to rental prices, that the former could soar while the latter remained nearly flat.

The level of incompetence in high places was and is truly astounding. The *Wall Street Journal* recently reported that mortgage analysts were tracking the rise in delinquencies and foreclosures in 2007 and 2008 and wondering whether they would follow the same pattern as in 2001 and 2002, when they started to level off and eventually fell.[3] House prices were rising at double-digit annual rates in 2001 and 2002. They were falling at double-digit rates at the end of 2007 and the beginning of 2008. Common sense suggests that such extrapolations are useless, but highly paid mortgage analysts are trying to make them.

If these economic and financial analysts were competent in their jobs, they would not have held beliefs about the markets they analyze that do not make sense. The experts in government, academia, and business who failed to see these bubbles and warn of their dangers were seriously negligent in performing their duties. The country is suffering enormous pain because these bubbles were allowed to grow unchecked. To prevent similar episodes of incompetence in the future, there should be some professional consequence for those who failed in such a significant way.

In the absence of serious consequences for poor performance, experts have little incentive to question the consensus view. During the bubble years, those who raised questions about bubbles were largely marginalized. Some analysts at major brokerage firms lost their jobs in the late 1990s because they advised clients that the run-up in stock prices wouldn't continue and would even be partially reversed. Similarly, during the years from 2004 to 2006, the major Wall Street banks were earning enormous profits based on the growth in the market for new derivative instruments. Those who raised questions about the safety of these instruments probably didn't win promotions and bonuses.

The bailouts of financial institutions provide an opportunity to apply sanctions to failed managers and experts. A standard condition for any bailout ought to be that the top managers who brought their financial institutions to bankruptcy should be removed. Given the bloated salaries in these institutions, the next echelon of managers should be forced to take large pay cuts as well. Given that these firms are bankrupt, and therefore almost by definition had poor management, there seems little reason to fear that these managers might leave and even many reasons to hope that they will.

In no other sector of the economy is pay for top executives more bloated than on Wall Street, and nowhere is compensation less connected to performance. Many of the big actors in the housing bubble will walk away with tens to hundreds of millions of dollars for creating a problem that has done such enormous harm to millions of American households and shareholders. Serious compensation restrictions as a condition of any assistance, including borrowing from the Fed's discount window, would be a huge step toward reining in executive compensation in the financial sector.

The government can and should go even further by placing restrictions on executive compensation as a condition of doing any public business, such as underwriting bond issues or managing pension money. If the Wall Street crew find such conditions too onerous, many financial institutions around the world would eagerly jump in to fill the gap and probably do a much better job.

Ideally, the laws of corporate governance would be rewritten to rein in executive compensation more generally. Coordinating a diverse group of shareholders to prevent the insiders from raiding the corporate trough is difficult. If the rules of governance were rewritten to require that executive compensation packages be clearly communicated to and approved by shareholders at regular intervals, these packages would likely be brought down to earth.

The exorbitant pay received by top executives is passed on in higher prices to everyone. It also distorts pay scales throughout the economy. Top managers in government, universities, and even private charities demand pay based on the seven-, eight-, and nine-figure compensation packages received by the top executives in major corporations. Curbing the pay of top corporate executives would restore greater equality throughout the economy.

MITIGATING THE PAIN
OF THE HOUSING COLLAPSE

There's no way to avoid considerable hardship when the economy loses $8 trillion of housing wealth. However, the government can lessen the pain with well-crafted policies.

To boost the economy out of the downturn caused by the crash, we need a stimulus. Initially this stimulus should take the form of large increases in government spending to sustain demand; however, over the longer term, an increase in net exports through a lower-valued dollar will be required. Reducing the value of the dollar should be a top goal of economic policy. The recent run-up in the dollar will have to be reversed; additional declines against Asian currencies will be needed. Ideally, the decline in the dollar will be negotiated, but the United States has the power to lower the value of the dollar, and it should be prepared to do so if negotiations prove futile.

Homeowners can't be compensated for the loss of equity, but the government can help people remain in their homes. The most obvious step would be changing the rules on foreclosure to give homeowners facing that possibility the option of remaining in their homes as long-term renters, paying the market rent.[4] A temporary change in foreclosure rules along these lines could be made immediately at no cost to the government and with no additional government bureaucracy.

Such a change would alter the incentive structure for lenders. If foreclosure no longer gives them the option of getting tenant-free possession of the house, lenders have far more incentive to renegotiate terms on a mortgage in order to allow the homeowners to remain in their homes as owners. Such a measure would make this an option for a large share of the people currently facing foreclosure.

In general, housing policy should shift away from an ideological bias that says that homeownership is desirable at all costs. Specifically, a more balanced assessment of the relative merits of renting and ownership is needed. Homeownership is often a good vehicle for families to accumulate wealth and obtain secure housing. However, it will not everywhere and always be the best route toward either goal. Housing policy must recognize that for many people, renting provides the better option for at least some of their lives.

Therefore, housing policy should be designed to provide good secure rental options to families. People shouldn't be treated as second-class citizens simply because they're renters. The ideology of homeownership was a big factor pushing families, including many low- and moderate-income families, into purchasing homes at bubble-inflated prices in the 2003–2007 period. Many of these families ended up losing their modest life savings and in some cases were forced to lose their homes, go bankrupt, or both. It would be truly tragic if the policymakers who touted the homeownership-first ideology refused to reexamine their views and picked up where they left off, potentially putting another cohort of new homeowners at risk.

CHAPTER 7

Learning from the Bubbles

The stock market and housing bubbles were the central features of the U.S. economy over the last 15 years. The stock bubble propelled the strongest period of economic growth since the late 1960s. The housing bubble lifted the economy from the wreckage of the stock bubble and sustained a modest recovery, at least through 2007. However, financial bubbles by definition aren't sustainable, and when they collapse, they cause enormous social and economic damage.

The economy had no problem with financial bubbles during its period of strongest and most evenly shared growth, the years from 1945 to 1973. It only became susceptible to bubbles after the pattern of growth had broken down—when most workers no longer shared in the benefits of productivity growth, and businesses no longer routinely invested to meet increased demand based on growing consumption. We don't have enough evidence to say that bubbles are a direct outgrowth of inequality, but, again, we do know that bubbles weren't a problem when income was more evenly distributed.

The bubbles were allowed to grow only because the people in a position to restrain them failed in their duties. The leading villain in this story is Alan Greenspan. Greenspan mastered the art of currying the favor of the rich and powerful and held top economic positions under five presidents of both political parties. He also managed to gain a near cult-like following among the media. As a result, most of the public is largely unaware of how disastrous the Fed's policies under his tenure were for the economy and the country.

Most of the economics profession went along for the ride, somehow managing to miss a $10 trillion stock bubble in the 1990s and an $8 trillion housing bubble in the current decade. If leading economists had recognized these bubbles and expressed concern about the inherent risks, they could have alerted the public and forced a serious policy debate on the problem. Instead, the leading voices in the profession joined the chorus of Greenspan sycophants, honoring him as potentially the greatest central banker of all time.

The financial industry proved to be more incompetent and corrupt than its worst critics could have imagined. Did people who manage multi-billion dollar portfolios in the late 1990s

really believe that price-to-earnings ratios would continue rising, even when they already exceeded 30 to 1? Or did these
highly paid fund managers believe that PE ratios no longer
mattered—as though people bought up shares of stock because the stock certificates were pretty?

It's hard to understand how anyone who managed money
for a living could have justified keeping a substantial portion
of their funds in the ridiculously overvalued markets of 1999
and 2000. You could play the bubble, riding the wave up and
dumping stock before the crash. But a buy-and-hold strategy
in 1999 and 2000 was a guaranteed loser. In the late 1990s,
Warren Buffet famously commented that he didn't understand the Internet economy, and thus he pulled much of his
portfolio out of the market. Buffet understood the Internet
economy very well. He recognized a hugely overvalued stock
market that was certain to crash. Why didn't fund managers?

The financial industry's conduct in the housing bubble was
even worse. House prices had sharply diverged from a 100-year
trend without any explanation. Furthermore, vacancy rates
were at record highs and getting higher. In introductory economics, we teach students about supply and demand. If the
excess supply keeps growing, what will happen to the price?
Furthermore, inflation-adjusted rents weren't rising through
most of the period of the housing bubble. There will always
be a rough balance between sales price and rent. When sales

prices diverge sharply from rents, some owners become renters, reducing the demand for housing. Similarly, some owners of rental units convert them to ownership units, increasing the supply of housing.

Decreased demand and increased supply lowers the price; what part of that reality did the highly compensated analysts fail to understand? How could the CEOs of the country's two huge mortgage giants, Fannie Mae and Freddie Mac, have been surprised by the housing bubble? The Wall Street wizards at Merrill Lynch, Citigroup, Bear Stearns, and elsewhere were probably even worse. Did they really have no idea that the bubble would burst and that a large amount of mortgage debt, especially subprime mortgage debt, would become nearly worthless? Did they think that this junk could be made to disappear through complex derivative instruments?

Wall Street sold these instruments to pension funds and other institutional investors. It also persuaded state and local governments to pay them billions of dollars in fees for issuing auction rate securities and for buying credit default swaps and other exotic financial instruments. In addition, many of the same institutional investors lost billions of dollars by holding the stock of companies like Merrill Lynch, Citigroup, and Bear Stearns, the value of which was driven into the ground by very highly paid executives.

The real problem is that the public, including many of the

pension fund managers who were taken for a ride, still don't understand what has happened. Perhaps the main reason for this confusion has been the quality of economic reporting. The media relied almost exclusively on the folks who got it wrong. The industry bubble-pushers and the bubble-deniers in policy positions were almost the only sources for economic reporting during the bubble years. The vast majority of the people who follow the news probably never heard anyone argue that the economy was being driven by a stock bubble in the 1990s or a housing bubble in the current decade. Such views simply were not permitted. (The *New York Times* deserves special mention as a media outlet that actively sought alternative voices, especially during the housing bubble.)

Knowingly or not, these outlets have covered up the extraordinary incompetence and corruption that allowed these bubbles to grow. For example, in a recent three-part series on the housing bubble, the *Washington Post* reported a claim from Alan Greenspan that he first became aware of the explosion in subprime mortgage lending as he was about to leave his post as Fed chair in January of 2006.[1] According to the article, Greenspan said he couldn't remember if he had passed this information on to his successor, Ben Bernanke.

This article makes it sound as though the explosion in subprime lending was an obscure piece of data only available to a privileged few. In reality, the explosion in subprime lending was a widely discussed feature of the housing market during the bubble years. If Greenspan was implying that he was unaware of this explosion, he was unbelievably negligent in his job as Fed chair. The notion that Greenspan would have to pass this information on to his successor—as though an economist of Bernanke's stature could be unaware of such an important development in the economy—is equally absurd. In other words, the *Post* article helped Greenspan present a remarkably straightforward development—namely, the massive issuance of bad loans—as complex and confusing.

In the same vein, the *Wall Street Journal* provided cover for Treasury Secretary Henry Paulson by explaining how the collapse of Fannie Mae and Freddie Mac caught him by surprise.[2] These two financial institutions hold almost nothing except mortgages and mortgage-backed securities. What did Mr. Paulson think would happen to them in a housing crash?

The secret of these two bubbles is that there is no secret. Anyone with common sense, a grasp of simple arithmetic, and a willingness to stand up against the consensus could have figured out the basic story. The details of the accounting scandals in the stock bubble and the convoluted financing stories in the housing bubble required some serious investigative work, but the bubbles themselves were there in plain sight for all to see.

The public should demand a real accounting. Why does the Fed grow hysterical over a 2.5 percent inflation rate but think that $10 trillion financial bubbles can be ignored? Where was the Treasury Department during the Clinton and Bush administrations? What about congressional oversight? Did no one in Congress think that massive bubbles might pose a problem? Why do economists worry so much more about small tariffs on steel and shirts than about gigantic financial bubbles? What exactly do the people who get paid millions of dollars by Wall Street financial firms do for their money? And finally, why don't the business and economic reporters ask any of these questions?

The stock and housing bubbles have wreaked havoc on the economy and will cause enormous pain for years to come. We can't undo the damage, but we can try to create a system that will prevent such catastrophes from recurring and that ensures that people responsible for these preventable events are held accountable. That would be a huge step forward.

Notes

CHAPTER 1

1. These data are taken from the *Economic Report of the President*, various years.

2. Data on car ownership rates are available in *The Statistical Abstract of the United States*, Bureau of the Census, various years.

3. Board of Governors of the Federal Reserve Board, Flow of Funds Table L.213.

4. This is taken from the home price component from the Bureau of Labor Statistics' consumer price index.

5. David Vogel, *Fluctuating Fortunes: The Political Power of Business in the United States* (New York: Basic Books, 1989).

6. The data on CEO pay are taken from Lawrence Mishel, Jared Bernstein, and Sylvia Allegretto, "The State of Working America, 2006–2007," Economic Policy Institute, 2006, 202. The data on wages at different points along the wage distribution can

be found on the Economic Policy Institute's website at www.epi
.org/content.cfm/datazone_dznational.

CHAPTER 2

1. Robert Reich, *Locked in the Cabinet* (New York: Vintage
Press, 1998), 65.

2. Council of Economic Advisors, *Economic Report of the President, 1994* (Washington, DC: U.S. Government Printing Office,
1994), 86–87.

3. Ibid, 85.

4. This deal is described in Bob Woodward's book, *The
Agenda: Inside the Clinton White House* (New York: Simon Schuster, 1994).

5. Greenspan's logic actually made no sense. Productivity
growth is equal to the growth in GDP minus the growth in hours
worked. No one claimed that hours were being mismeasured,
so if productivity growth was being mismeasured, GDP growth
was also. Therefore, if Greenspan was right about the measurement issue, GDP was already growing more rapidly than the data
showed.

6. For example, see Sam Beard, *Restoring Hope in America: The
Social Security Solution* (Richmond, CA: ICS Press, 1996).

7. See Dean Baker, *Saving Social Security with Stock: The
Promises Don't Add Up*, (New York: Twentieth Century Fund
and Economic Policy Institute, 1997); and Dean Baker, J. Bradford DeLong, and Paul Krugman, "Asset Returns and Economic
Growth," *Brookings Papers on Economic Activity* 1 (2005):
289–330.

CHAPTER 3

1. The details for this scam can be found in David D. Kirkpatrick, "Guilty Pleas Are Expected at Homestore," *New York Times*, September 25, 2002.

2. Agis Salpukas, "Firing Up An Idea Machine; Enron Is Encouraging the Entrepreneurs Within," *New York Times*, June, 27, 1999.

3. *Economic Report of the President*, 2004, Table B.

4. Alan Greenspan, "Outlook for the Federal Budget and Implications for Fiscal Policy," testimony before the Committee on the Budget, U.S. Senate, January 25, 2001, www.federalreserve .gov/boarddocs/testimony/2001/20010125/default.htm.

5. Corporations often pay much of their profits back to shareholders in the form of share buybacks. This has the effect of boosting share prices. Higher share prices are often preferred by shareholders to dividends, because dividends are subject to income taxes, while the rise in share prices is not, unless the stock is sold. Even in that case, the shareholder will pay only the tax on capital gains, which have generally been lower than the tax rate on dividends and other ordinary income.

CHAPTER 4

1. These calculations use the average house price from the Census Bureau's American Community Survey for 2006 and adjust it in accordance with the changes in the Case-Shiller index over the same period. Average prices refer to metropolitan areas, the cities themselves.

2. Kirstin Downey, "Doors Close for Real Estate Speculators; After Pushing Up Prices, Investors Are Left Holding Too Many Homes," *Washington Post*, April 22, 2006.

3. *Washington Post*, "Making It; A Wife Is Still out of Reach, but He Can Almost Touch Retirement," September 3, 2006.

4. Alan Greenspan, "Monetary Policy and the Economic Outlook," testimony before the Joint Economic Committee, U.S. Congress, April 17, 2002, www.federalreserve.gov/boarddocs/ testimony/2002/20020417/default.htm.

5. Dean Baker, "The Run-Up in House Prices: Is It Real or Is It Another Bubble?" *Center for Economic and Policy Research* (Washington DC), 2002.

6. This can be calculated by tying together the old home price series from the consumer price index published by the Bureau of Labor Statistics with the Housing Price Index (HPI) from OFHEO.

7. Jonathan McCarthy and Richard W. Peach. "Are Home Prices the Next 'Bubble'?" *Economic Policy Review*, Federal Reserve Board of New York, December, 2004.

8. Dean Baker. "Too Much Bubbly at the Fed? The New York Federal Reserve Board's Analysis of the Run-Up in Home Prices," *Center for Economic and Policy Research* (Washington DC), July 2004, www.cepr.net/index.php/publications/reports/ too-much-bubbly-at-the-fed/.

9. This data can be found in Federal Reserve Board's Flow of Funds data, Table B.100, Line 50, www.federalreserve.gov/ releases/z1/Current/z1r-5.pdf.

CHAPTER 5

1. There's a long history of discrimination in bank lending, with African Americans and Latinos being charged higher interest rates or being denied access to credit altogether.

2. CreditSights, "Wachovia One-on-One: Lessons Learned in Mortgage Land," 2008, CreditSights Inc.

3. David S. Hilzenrath, "Fannie's Perilous Pursuit of Subprime Loans," *Washington Post*, August 19, 2008, D1.

4. These figures are taken from T2 Partners LLC, "Why We Are Still in the Early Innings of the Bursting of the Housing and Credit Bubbles and Its Implications for MBIA and Ambac," T2 Partners, LLC (New York), 2008.

5. Roger Lowenstein, "Triple-A Failure," *New York Times Magazine*, April 27, 2008. This article provides an interesting account of how the credit-rating agencies struggled with the new financial instruments that fueled the housing bubble.

6. Ibid.

7. Bank of International Settlements, "Triennial and Semi-annual Surveys on Positions in Global Over-the-Counter Derivatives Markets as of the End of June, 2007," Table A, www.bis.org/publ/otc_hy0711.pdf?noframes=1.

8. For a fascinating account on the sale of a related instrument, interest rate swaps, to the Erie, Pennsylvania School District, see Martin Z. Braun and William Selway, "Hidden Swap Fees by JP Morgan, Morgan Stanley Hit School Boards," February 1, 2008, www.bloomberg.com/apps/news?pid=newsarchive&sid=ay5LDb jbjy6c.

9. Ben Bernanke, "Testimony before the Joint Economic Com-

mittee," U.S. Congress, March 28, 2007, www.federalreserve.gov/newsevents/testimony/bernanke20070328a.htm.

10. An alternative interpretation is that the Fed wanted to prop up banks that were genuinely insolvent, and they knew that the market would recognize their insolvency if they borrowed from the discount window, effectively causing a bank run. The implication of this view is that the Fed was directly using taxpayer dollars to subsidize banks that should have failed.

11. Vikas Bijaj, "Top Lender Sees Mortgage Woes for 'Good' Risks," *New York Times*, July 25, 2007.

12. *Washington Post,* "To Blunt a Recession: Fiscal Stimulus May Eventually Be Needed, but There Are Pitfalls," editorial, January 11, 2008, A16.

13. *Washington Post*, editorial, January 19, 2008, A20.

14. Thomas Friedman, "Rescue the Rescue," *New York Times*, September 30, 2008.

15. See, for example, Heather Landy, "New Law Seeks to Limit Executive Compensation," *Washington Post*, October 4, 2008, D1.

16. Dean Baker and David Rosnick, "The Housing Crash and the Retirement Prospects of the Late Bay Boomers," *Center for Economic and Policy Research* (Washington DC), 2008, www.cepr.net/index.php/publications/reports/the-housing-crash-and-the-retirement-prospects-of-late-baby-boomers/.

CHAPTER 6

1. This comment was made at a meeting of central bankers in Jackson Hole, Wyoming. Richard W. Stevenson, "Policy Makers

Hone Debate: When to Hold, When to Fold," *New York Times*, September 3, 2002, C1.

2. See Robert Pollin, Dean Baker, and Marc Schaberg, "Financial Transactions Taxes for the U.S. Economy," *Political Economy Research Institute* (University of Massachusetts, Amherst, MA), 2002, www.peri.umass.edu/236/hash/aef97d8d65/publication/172/.

3. Liam Pleven, "What's Subprime's Magic Number?" *Wall Street Journal*, May 3, 2008.

4. This proposal is outlined in "The Subprime Borrower Protection Plan," by Dean Baker, *Economic and Policy Research* (Washington DC), 2007, www.cepr.net/index.php/op-cds-columns/op-eds-columns/the-subprime-borrower-protection-plan/]. A version of this proposal was introduced as the "Saving Family Homes Act" by Representative Raul Grijalva (D-AZ) earlier this year, www.govtrack.us/congress/bill.xpd?bill=h110-6116].

CHAPTER 7

1. *Washington Post*, "Anatomy of a Meltdown: The Credit Crisis, Part I," June 15, 2008, A1.

2. *Wall Street Journal*, "Fannie and Freddie Test Paulson's Grit," September 1, 2008, A1.

Glossary

adjustable-rate mortgage (ARM). A mortgage with an
interest rate that changes depending on market interest
rates. Typically, ARMs are reset every year depending on the
market interest rates in the three-month period prior to the
reset date.

all-stock transaction. A transaction—most often a corporate
takeover—in which stock is used in lieu of cash to purchase
another company.

arbitrage bets. Trades that take advantage of differences
in price that are not expected to persist. For example, if the
dollar trades for more in London than in New York, an
"arbitrager" would buy dollars in New York and sell them in

London. This activity will quickly eliminate any differences in price when carried out on a large scale.

auction rate security. Typically a municipal or corporate bond whose interest rate is reset at regular intervals, sometimes as often as every 7 days, but more typically at intervals of around 30 days. Borrowers can benefit if short-term rates remain lower than long-term rates and their credit rating does not deteriorate. However, an auction rate security subjects the borrower to much greater risk than when a long-term rate is locked in through a normal bond issue.

baseline path. A projection for the economy or the budget that assumes there will be no changes to current policy.

commodities. Products that can be sold in large quantities without important qualitative variations. Commodities consist primarily of agricultural goods and raw materials, as well as some basic industrial inputs, such as steel or lumber.

corporate governance structure. The rules and bodies that control corporate behavior, including the top corporate management and the board of directors, as well as the mechanisms through which such structures are held accountable to shareholders and possibly other stakeholders, such as employees.

credit default swaps. A type of insurance against bond defaults. Use of this newly created instrument exploded during the years of the housing bubble. The issuer of a credit default swap agrees to pay the holder in the event that there is a default on the insured bond. The bonds covered include corporate and government bonds and mortgage-backed securities.

defined-benefit pension plan. A pension plan that guarantees workers a fixed monthly benefit based on their earnings during their working years.

derivative instruments. Financial instruments that derive their value by being tied to other instruments. For example, an option on currency is a derivative instrument because it gives its holder the right to buy currency at a certain price at a date in the future.

derivative markets. The markets for trading derivative instruments. In some cases, for example options and futures on commodities, there are well-developed exchanges, such as the Chicago Board of Trade. However, in other cases, most notably credit default swaps, the markets usually consist of trades directly between banks and other actors.

EBITDA (earnings before interest, taxes, depreciation and amortization). A category of earning that became popular during the height of the stock bubble. It was not a well-defined accounting category, which meant that companies had considerable leeway in calculating their EBITDA.

federal funds rate. The interest rate that banks charge each other to borrow money overnight in order to meet their reserve requirement. This rate is most directly under the control of the Federal Reserve Board and is its main instrument for controlling the economy.

financial sector. The sector of the economy that includes banks, insurance companies, real estate companies, and other businesses whose primary activity involves mediating between the buying and selling of items as opposed to directly providing a good or service.

GDP (gross domestic product). The total value of goods and services produced by the economy over a period of time.

hedge funds. Investment funds that operate outside most regulatory structures. Hedge funds are not subject to the disclosure requirements of mutual funds, pension funds, or most other pools of capital.

inflationary spiral. A process whereby inflation continually increases, with wages rising in response to higher prices, and higher wages forcing prices even higher. In extreme cases, this process can lead to hyperinflation and an economic collapse.

leverage. The amount of an investment made with borrowed money. For example, if a person buys a house with a 10 percent down payment, she has leveraged her money at a rate of 10 to 1, with the purchase price equal to 10 times the down payment.

LBOs (leveraged buyouts). The takeover of a company that relies on borrowed money, often 90 percent or more of the purchase price. Borrowing can occur through bond issues and bank loans.

margin requirement. The limit often imposed by the Federal Reserve Board to the extent brokerage houses can allow their customers to borrow money to buy stock. Margin borrowing is using borrowed money to buy stock.

market capitalization. The market value of the shares of a company at a point in time.

mortgage-backed securities. Bonds that are backed by a set of mortgages. These bonds will typically involve claims on the interest, the principle, or both of hundreds of mortgages. These claims in turn provide the basis for regular interest payments on mortgage-backed securities.

NAIRU (non-accelerating inflation rate of unemployment).
According to one theory of the economy, this rate of
unemployment is consistent with a stable rate of inflation.
For example, if the NAIRU is 6 percent, the inflation rate
will stay exactly at its current level if the unemployment rate
is also 6 percent. The inflation rate would increase if the
unemployment rate were to fall below 6 percent, and the
inflation rate would fall if the unemployment rate were to
rise above 6 percent.

options. The right to buy or sell an item, such as a commodity,
currency, or stock, at a specific price at a specific time.

panic selling. Selling of an asset motivated by fear instead of a
rational calculation of the asset's value.

perverse incentives. Incentives that encourage people to
engage in economically harmful activities. For example,
if mortgage issuers are paid for the number of mortgages
they issue, regardless of whether borrowers can repay the
mortgage, they will have incentive to issue mortgages that
can't be repaid.

PE (price-to-earnings ratio). The ratio of the price of a share
of stock to after-tax earnings per share.

productivity growth. The rate of increase in the value of output (goods and services) produced per hour of work.

secondary market. The market for reselling an asset after its original sale. For example, the stock market is a secondary market for reselling shares of stock after companies have originally sold them. In the mortgage market, the secondary market is where the issuer of the mortgage sells a mortgage.

trend levels. Levels that follow a set growth path, as opposed to fluctuating according to cyclical factors or other conditions. For example, if trend growth is 3 percent annually, the trend level will be 3 percent higher every year, regardless of actual growth.

windfall profits. Profits that had not been anticipated at the time an investment was made. For example, if an oil company makes investments expecting that the price of oil will be $50 a barrel and the price of oil is $150 a barrel, the additional $100 a barrel would be a windfall profit.

Acknowledgments

I have benefited enormously from exchanges with friends and colleagues with whom I have shared my obsession with the stock and housing bubbles. Several among this group stand out for putting up with more than their fair share of my writings. Particularly helpful were my colleagues at the Center for Economic and Policy Research: Heather Boushey, David Rosnick, John Schmitt, and Mark Weisbrot. Helene Jorgensen and Eileen Appelbaum also have given many insightful comments on my work over the years.

I also thank Helene, Walnut, Fulton, and Rufus for putting up with my neglect as I spent time working on this book and in other ways trying to attack the bubble economy.

Index

About the Author

Dean Baker is co-director of the Center for Economic and Policy Research in Washington DC. His weblog, "Beat the Press," appears on the *American Prospect* website and features commentary on economic reporting.

Baker's columns have appeared in many major media outlets, including the *Atlantic Monthly*, the *Washington Post*, and the *London Financial Times*. He is frequently cited in economics reporting in major media outlets, including the *New York Times*, the *Washington Post*, CNBC, and National Public Radio.

His previous books include *The United States since 1980* (2007), *The Conservative Nanny State: How the Wealthy Use the Government to Stay Rich and Get Richer* (2006), *Social Security: The Phony Crisis* (with Mark Weisbrot, 1999), *The*

Benefits of Full Employment (with Jared Bernstein, 2004), and *Getting Prices Right: The Battle Over the Consumer Price Index* (1997), which received a Choice Book Award as one of the outstanding academic books of the year.

Baker has served as a senior economist at the Economic Policy Institute, an assistant professor at Bucknell University, and a consultant for the World Bank, the Joint Economic Committee of the U.S. Congress, and the OECD's Trade Union Advisory Council. He wrote the Economic Reporting Review, the weekly online commentary on economic reporting, from 1996 to 2006. He received his Ph.D. in economics from the University of Michigan.

Other Books from PoliPointPress

The Blue Pages: A Directory of Companies Rated by Their Politics and Practices
Helps consumers match their buying decisions with their political values by listing the political contributions and business practices of over 1,000 companies. $9.95, paperback.

Rose Aguilar, *Red Highways: A Liberal's Journey into the Heartland*
Challenges red state stereotypes to reveal new strategies for progressives. $15.95, paperback.

Jeff Cohen, *Cable News Confidential: My Misadventures in Corporate Media*
Offers a fast-paced romp through the three major cable news channels—Fox CNN, and MSNBC—and delivers a serious message about their failure to cover the most urgent issues of the day. $14.95, paperback.

Marjorie Cohn, *Cowboy Republic: Six Ways the Bush Gang Has Defied the Law*
Shows how the executive branch under President Bush has systematically defied the law instead of enforcing it. $14.95, paperback.

Joe Conason, *The Raw Deal: How the Bush Republicans Plan to Destroy Social Security and the Legacy of the New Deal*
Reveals the well-financed and determined effort to undo the Social Security Act and other New Deal programs. $11.00, paperback.

Kevin Danaher and Alisa Gravitz, *Building the Green Economy: Success Stories from the Grassroots*
Shows how community groups, families, and individual citizens have protected their food and water, cleaned up their neighborhoods, and strengthened their local economies. $16.00, paperback.

Kevin Danaher, Shannon Biggs, and Jason Mark, *The Green Festival Reader: Fresh Ideas from Agents of Change*
Collects the best ideas and commentary from some of the most forward green thinkers of our time. $15.95, paperback.

Reese Erlich, *Dateline Havana: The Real Story of U.S. Policy and the Future of Cuba*
Explores Cuba's strained relationship with the United States, the island nation's evolving culture and politics, and prospects for U.S. Cuba policy with the departure of Fidel Castro. $22.95, hardcover.

Reese Erlich, *The Iran Agenda: The Real Story of U.S. Policy and the Middle East Crisis*
Explores the turbulent recent history between the two countries and how it has led to a showdown over nuclear technology. $14.95, paperback.

Steven Hill, *10 Steps to Repair American Democracy*
Identifies the key problems with American democracy, especially
election practices, and proposes ten specific reforms to reinvigorate it.
$11.00, paperback.

**Markos Kounalakis and Peter Laufer, *Hope Is a Tattered Flag: Voices
of Reason and Change for the Post-Bush Era***
Gathers together the most listened-to politicos and pundits, activists and
thinkers, to answer the question: what happens after Bush leaves office?
$29.95, hardcover; $16.95 paperback.

**Yvonne Latty, *In Conflict: Iraq War Veterans Speak Out on Duty, Loss,
and the Fight to Stay Alive***
Features the unheard voices, extraordinary experiences, and personal
photographs of a broad mix of Iraq War veterans, including Congressman
Patrick Murphy, Tammy Duckworth, Kelly Daugherty, and Camilo
Mejia. $24.00, hardcover.

**Phillip Longman, *Best Care Anywhere: Why VA Health Care Is Better
Than Yours***
Shows how the turnaround at the long-maligned VA hospitals provides
a blueprint for salvaging America's expensive but troubled health care
system. $14.95, paperback.

**Marcia and Thomas Mitchell, *The Spy Who Tried to Stop a War:
Katharine Gun and the Secret Plot to Sanction the Iraq Invasion***
Describes a covert operation to secure UN authorization for the Iraq
war and the furor that erupted when a young British spy leaked it.
$23.95, hardcover.

Susan Mulcahy, ed., *Why I'm a Democrat*
Explores the values and passions that make a diverse group of Americans
proud to be Democrats. $14.95, paperback.

**Christine Pelosi, *Campaign Boot Camp: Basic Training for
Future Leaders***
Offers a seven-step guide for successful campaigns and causes at all levels
of government. $15.95, paperback.

**William Rivers Pitt, *House of Ill Repute: Reflections on War, Lies, and
America's Ravaged Reputation***
Skewers the Bush Administration for its reckless invasions, warrantless
wiretaps, lethally incompetent response to Hurricane Katrina, and other
scandals and blunders. $16.00, paperback.

Sarah Posner, *God's Profits: Faith, Fraud, and the Republican Crusade for Values Voters*
Examines corrupt televangelists' ties to the Republican Party and unprecedented access to the Bush White House. $19.95, hardcover.

Nomi Prins, *Jacked: How "Conservatives" Are Picking Your Pocket—Whether You Voted for Them or Not*
Describes how the "conservative" agenda has affected your wallet, skewed national priorities, and diminished America—but not the American spirit. $12.00, paperback.

Cliff Schecter, *The Real McCain: Why Conservatives Don't Trust Him—And Why Independents Shouldn't*
Explores the gap between the public persona of John McCain and the reality of this would-be president. $14.95, hardcover.

Norman Solomon, *Made Love, Got War: Close Encounters with America's Warfare State*
Traces five decades of American militarism and the media's all-too-frequent failure to challenge it. $24.95, hardcover.

John Sperling et al., *The Great Divide: Retro vs. Metro America*
Explains how and why our nation is so bitterly divided into what the authors call Retro and Metro America. $19.95, paperback.

Daniel Weintraub, *Party of One: Arnold Schwarzenegger and the Rise of the Independent Voter*
Explains how Schwarzenegger found favor with independent voters, whose support has been critical to his success, and suggests that his bipartisan approach represents the future of American politics. $19.95, hardcover.

Curtis White, *The Spirit of Disobedience: Resisting the Charms of Fake Politics, Mindless Consumption, and the Culture of Total Work*
Debunks the notion that liberalism has no need for spirituality and describes a "middle way" through our red state/blue state political impasse. Includes three powerful interviews with John DeGraaf, James Howard Kunstler, and Michael Ableman. $24.00, hardcover.

For more information, please visit
www.p3books.com.

About This Book

This book is printed on Cascade Enviro100 Print paper. It contains 100 percent post-consumer fiber and is certified EcoLogo, Processed Chlorine Free, and FSC Recycled. For each ton used instead of virgin paper, we

Save the equivalent of 17 trees

Reduce air emissions by 2,098 pounds

Reduce solid waste by 1,081 pounds

Reduce the water used by 10,196 gallons

Reduce suspended particles in the water by 6.9 pounds

This paper is manufactured using biogas energy, reducing natural gas consumption by 2,748 cubic feet per ton of paper produced.

The book's printer, Malloy Incorporated, works with paper mills that are environmentally responsible, that do not source fiber from endangered forests, and that are third-party certified. Malloy prints with soy- and vegetable-based inks, and over 98 percent of the solid material they discard is recycled. Their water emissions are entirely safe for disposal into their municipal sanitary sewer system, and they work with the Michigan Department of Environmental Quality to ensure that their air emissions meet all environmental standards.

The Michigan Department of Environmental Quality has recognized Malloy as a Great Printer for their compliance with environmental regulations, written environmental policy, pollution prevention efforts, and pledge to share best practices with other printers. Their county Department of Planning and Environment has designated them a Waste Knot Partner for their waste prevention and recycling programs.